HELPING SURVIVORS OF AUTHORITARIAN PARENTS, SIBLINGS, AND PARTNERS

Helping Survivors of Authoritarian Parents, Siblings, and Partners considers the notion of the authoritarian personality in a family context and examines the extent to which authoritarians traumatize the people closest to them. Building on primary research, Dr. Maisel presents first-person accounts of life with authoritarian family members and provides clinicians and other professionals with tactics and strategies for helping clients who struggle with the impact of these experiences. This unique look at authoritarians at home serves to redefine the authoritarian personality, expand our understanding of family trauma, and give voice to the silent epidemic of authoritarian wounding.

Eric Maisel, PhD, is a retired licensed psychotherapist, active creativity coach, and internationally respected expert in the field of mental health reform. He is the author of more than fifty books, writes the "Rethinking Mental Health" blog for *Psychology Today*, and provides lectures and workshops worldwide.

HELPING SURVIVORS OF AUTHORITARIAN PARENTS, SIBLINGS, AND PARTNERS

A Guide for Professionals

Eric Maisel

Routledge
Taylor & Francis Group
NEW YORK AND LONDON

First published 2019
by Routledge
711 Third Avenue, New York, NY 10017

and by Routledge
2 Park Square, Milton Park, Abingdon, Oxon, OX14 4RN

Routledge is an imprint of the Taylor & Francis Group, an informa business

© 2019 Eric Maisel

The right of Eric Maisel to be identified as author of this work has been asserted by him in accordance with sections 77 and 78 of the Copyright, Designs and Patents Act 1988.

All rights reserved. No part of this book may be reprinted or reproduced or utilised in any form or by any electronic, mechanical, or other means, now known or hereafter invented, including photocopying and recording, or in any information storage or retrieval system, without permission in writing from the publishers.

Trademark notice: Product or corporate names may be trademarks or registered trademarks, and are used only for identification and explanation without intent to infringe.

Library of Congress Cataloging-in-Publication Data
Names: Maisel, Eric, 1947– author.
Title: Helping survivors of authoritarian parents, siblings, and partners: a guide for professionals / Eric Maisel.
Description: New York: Routledge, 2019. | Includes index.
Identifiers: LCCN 2018021277 (print) | LCCN 2018029573 (ebook) | ISBN 9781138498860 (hbk) | ISBN 9781138498877 (pbk) | ISBN 9780429507717 (ebk)
Subjects: LCSH: Authoritarianism (Personality trait) | Abusive parents. | Parent and child.
Classification: LCC BF698.35.A87 (ebook) | LCC BF698.35.A87 M35 2019 (print) | DDC 155.9/24—dc23
LC record available at https://lccn.loc.gov/2018021277

ISBN: 978-1-138-49886-0 (hbk)
ISBN: 978-1-138-49887-7 (pbk)
ISBN: 978-0-429-50771-7 (ebk)

Typeset in New Baskerville Std
by codeMantra

For Ann,
Forty years into this adventure

CONTENTS

1 Updating the Concept of the Authoritarian Personality 1

2 The Aggression Cluster 9

3 Please Break My Rules! 17

4 Walking on Eggshells 25

5 I. Hate. My. Mother. 32

6 Perfection Was the Minimum 39

7 Whole Scarred Families 46

8 The Exploitation Cluster 53

9 Exploiting Ignorance 61

10 Exploiting Religion and Religiosity 69

11 Some Cat Toys and Freedom 77

12 My Hansel and Gretel Life 83

13 The Narcissism Cluster 90

14 Narcissism, Conventionality, and Passivity 98

CONTENTS

15	Killing the Family Dog	105
16	Consequences: Depression	112
17	Consequences: Anxiety	119
18	Consequences: Addiction	130
19	Consequences: Physical Complaints	137
20	Consequences: Repetition Compulsion	144
21	What You Can Expect	151
22	Bringing Up Authoritarian Wounding	158
23	Trauma-Informed Care	165
24	Existential Care	173
25	Interpersonal, Relational, and Family Help	181
26	Tips for Dealing with an Authoritarian Parent	188
27	Supporting Physical and Emotional Separation	195
28	My 15 Learnings	202
	Appendix: Authoritarian Wound Questionnaire	209
	Index	213

1

UPDATING THE CONCEPT OF THE AUTHORITARIAN PERSONALITY

My goals for this book are to update the concept of the authoritarian personality based on the experiences of victims of authoritarian contact, describe what victims of authoritarian wounding endure, and explain what you can do in session to help heal these authoritarian wounds. I think that you will find this important because many of your clients, and maybe even the majority of them, are survivors of authoritarian wounding who need your help.

The "authoritarian personality" is a relatively recent concept. Starting in the 1950s, a body of research focused on trying to understand why so many ordinary folks were quick to act cruelly, easy in meting out severe punishment to both loved ones and strangers, eager to follow tyrants on the right or the left, and more concerned about appearances than in doing the moral thing. Distinctions were made between authoritarian followers and authoritarian leaders, and the research tended to concern itself with the former, since they appeared to make up the bulk of authoritarians.

Following the cataclysmic events of World War II, researchers attempted to identify the qualities, characteristics, beliefs, and behaviors of authoritarian leaders, authoritarian followers, authoritarian parents, and those other folks who, in one social psychology experiment after another, displayed an easily accessible inhumanity. These researchers included Theodor Adorno and his colleagues at the University of California at Berkeley, who in the 1950s coined the phrase "the authoritarian personality," as well as Stanley Milgram and his famous learning experiments and the contemporary Canadian psychologist Bob Altemeyer, whose decades of research provided an unparalleled look into what he dubbed "right-wing authoritarianism."

The seminal research on and thinking about the authoritarian personality was conducted primarily by psychoanalytically inclined sociologists at UC Berkeley. The name most associated with that research is Theodor Adorno. These thinkers believed that they had identified nine characteristics of the authoritarian personality (or, more precisely, nine characteristics of the authoritarian follower):

1 Conventionalism: rigid adherence to conventional middle-class values
2 Authoritarian submission: uncritical acceptance of authority
3 Authoritarian aggression: a tendency to condemn anyone who violates conventional norms
4 Anti-intraception: a rejection of weakness or sentimentality
5 Superstition and stereotypy: belief in mystical determinants of action and rigid, categorical thinking
6 Power and toughness: preoccupation with dominance over others
7 Destructiveness and cynicism: a generalized feeling of hostility and anger
8 Projectivity: a tendency to project inner emotions and impulses outward
9 Sex: exaggerated concern for proper sexual conduct

The Canadian psychologist Bob Altemeyer, who spent his career researching various aspects of the authoritarian personality, identified three characteristics of typical North American authoritarian followers: authoritarian submission, authoritarian aggression, and conventionalism. In the 1960s, developmental psychologist Diana Baumrind, reporting on her research with preschool-age children, described three parenting styles, one of which came to be known as the authoritarian parenting style.

This style she described as characterized by strict rules, a refusal to explain the rules, the demand that these rules be followed unconditionally, and harsh punishment if they weren't followed.

Various lines of inquiry attempted to explain where this authoritarianism came from, using popular theories of the moment, for example, psychoanalytic theories in the 1950s and social learning theories in the 1960s. What no one thought to do was to ask the following simple question of people at large: if you've had contact with an authoritarian, taking "authoritarian" to mean whatever you take it to mean, what was your experience like? I've remedied this shortfall by widely administering an Authoritarian Wound Questionnaire to people from all walks of life.

I asked respondents to describe what they experienced from their contact with an authoritarian, to what extent they were wounded by that contact, and what they'd done to try to heal from that wounding. Respondents, it turned out, had a great deal to share and were grateful for the opportunity to tell their stories. The following emerged from their stories:

- Huge numbers of individuals have had painful, traumatic contact with an authoritarian. In my large sample, these authoritarians were as often female as male (that is, as often a mother as a father, as often a grandmother as a grandfather, etc.)
- Respondents reported more than 30 particular authoritarian traits and behaviors that clustered into three categories: an aggression cluster, an exploitation cluster, and a narcissism cluster.
- Their reports helped clarify what heretofore had been a murky distinction between authoritarian leader and authoritarian follower. Rather than there being two distinct types of authoritarians, what emerges is the portrait of a person who is both types at once, a dictator at home and more passive, meek, and submissive in the world. This

"two-faced" authoritarian is perhaps *the* typical authoritarian personality
- Respondents routinely reported significant negative outcomes resulting from this contact, from lifelong despair and anxiety to low self-esteem and self-sabotaging behaviors.
- Respondents also regularly reported that these issues, as profound as they were, seldom got addressed in therapy or counseling. In large part because therapists and counselors are not trained to ask directly about authoritarian wounding, this important subject tended to fly under the radar.
- Many respondents reported at least partial healing from that toxic contact. They virtually all named as their most important survival tactic getting away from the authoritarian. Because this is such an important matter, we'll spend an entire chapter on how you can help your clients achieve guilt-free separation, if such separation proves necessary.

In inaugurating this research, I wanted to let the victims of authoritarian wounding speak for themselves. Sometimes only briefly and sometimes at great length, respondents make an effort to describe their experiences and make sense of those experiences. What emerges is a snapshot of an everyday reality: the reality that many people among us – maybe even most of us – are obliged to deal with someone who displays certain toxic attitudes and behaviors, attitudes and behaviors that cause long-term harm. There are real authoritarians out there and real authoritarian victims out there – and you will encounter both in your practice. This book will help you deal with those victims.

Research on the authoritarian personality has typically focused on the authoritarian follower, that is, on the person who willingly embraces fascism when fascism appears. But the distinction between authoritarian follower and authoritarian leader is made cloudy by the following previous research shortfall. Because the victims of authoritarian wounding weren't queried on the subject, we didn't know how often the authoritarian in question acted like an authoritarian leader – bullying, exploitative, and narcissistic – at home and acted like an authoritarian follower – passive, meek, and pliable – in the world. Given this research, that reality is much clearer.

Sometimes the authoritarian was his or her bullying, cruel self in both places, both at home and in the world. But more often he or she showed two distinct faces, a punishing face at home and a submissive face in the world. Given these new findings, we may want to reevaluate the concept of the authoritarian personality and add this "new" two-faced authoritarian, where an essentially cruel person who is also frightened and weak is savvy enough and manipulative enough not to expose himself or herself as a bully or a sadist in public.

It is probably the case that the average authoritarian is both an authoritarian leader and an authoritarian follower, which helps explain why the victims of authoritarian wounding are often so confused and downright mystified by the authoritarian they are currently obliged to deal with or had to deal with in the past. That authoritarian looks one way in a private setting and another, virtually completely different way in a public setting. In addition to the other wounding effects of their contact with an authoritarian, your clients must deal with the effects of this profound confusion. It is no wonder that victims of authoritarian wounding report that they are *still* confused, both when it comes to making choices or doing intellectual work and in their understanding of the exact nature of their authoritarian wounding.

Authoritarians often look good in the world, even very good. They can be charming in public and expert at reserving their authoritarian wounding for family members. This conscious, calculated duplicity is a feature of an authoritarian's cynical desire to get what he or she wants – primarily the ability to inflict punishment – without experiencing negative consequences. Some authoritarians are authoritarian everywhere and easy to spot because they are cruel and dictatorial wherever they go. But others look absolutely wonderful in public, and it's only behind closed doors that they wreak their havoc.

This two-facedness is very important to understand. It helps explain why a person whom we might dub an authoritarian follower and who looks passive and unaggressive at first glance is so willing to act cruelly given the chance. Consider the following: when the Canadian psychologist Bob Altemeyer gathered together high-scoring authoritarians for an experiment that mimicked Stanley Milgram's famous learning experiment, inviting them to administer electroshock to a "learner" who wasn't learning properly, 100% of them administered the maximum electroshock available. (Of course, no shock was actually delivered.)

Reflect on that number: 100%.

Experimental settings of this sort provide a perfect storm opportunity for authoritarians to show who they really are. Would *you* administer what appears to be near-lethal electroshock to a stranger just because he seems not to be learning a trivial lesson properly? Presumably not, because you aren't filled with this same reservoir of hatred that looks to fill authoritarians, because you don't have their pressing need to punish, and because you possess humane values and principles. By contrast, subjects in countless experiments inflicted outsized punishment easily, without breaking a sweat and without any pangs of conscience. They were *primed to punish*, and they found the poor victim a suitable recipient of their ambient hatred.

This likely connects to the following. Also linked to the concept of the authoritarian personality is what psychologists have described as the "dark triad" of personality traits – narcissism, Machiavellianism, and psychopathy – a triad meant to capture the essence of a person who is callous, manipulative, cynical, deceptive, and remorseless. My sense is that this comes closer to describing an authoritarian's personality than does a definition that focuses on his or her desire for order, security, or power. It is an authoritarian's cruel nature, with its large portions of sadism and grandiosity, that defines him or her.

Whether publicly aggressive or publicly passive, the typical authoritarian looks to be fueled by hatred and a powerful need to punish. Anyone who has lived with an authoritarian, been employed by an authoritarian, or come into contact with an authoritarian political leader or religious leader senses that person's fundamental nature: the reservoir of spite, the need to belittle and ridicule, an appetite for control, and, especially, an insatiable desire to punish. Whether that individual is politically on the right or politically on the left, whether he or she professes to be religious or atheistic, what they share with their authoritarian brothers and sisters is a cruel, punishing nature, a lack of guilt and shame, and the cluster of traits and qualities we'll examine shortly.

Over the next several chapters we'll look at these three clusters of traits and qualities: the aggression cluster, the exploitation cluster, and the narcissism cluster. I'm presenting these ideas in detail so that you can get a better sense of what your clients have experienced, more clues as to what you might expect in session, and a clearer picture of what might help. Note that I've included "what you might expect in session." Authoritarian wounds are bound to play themselves out in session.

To take just one example, consider the matter of rules. Authoritarians use rules as part of their aggression agenda. They create quixotic, unclear, so-called rules just so that their victims will violate them and provide them with a rationale for punishing them. This unexplored dynamic is very important for you as a helper to understand, because your wounded clients are likely still in a perplexed and perplexing relationship to rules, including any rules that you set up for the therapy, the counseling, or the coaching. That will matter as you try to proceed with the work.

Remember that your clients who have been subjected to authoritarian wounding have been seriously harmed. We have words like "trauma" and phrases like "adverse childhood experiences" to describe harm of this sort. One of the goals of this book is to add "authoritarian wounding" to the list of known traumas and known adverse childhood experiences. We are understanding better all the time the extent to which trauma is significantly damaging. For example, according to one US Department of Health report, 55% to 99% of women in substance abuse treatment and 85% to 95% of women in the public mental health system reported a history of trauma. That's why, when we get to how you might prove of help, we will spend real time on the idea of trauma-informed care.

What looks to be at the heart of the authoritarian personality – whether that individual is a so-to-speak leader, follower, or, most often, both – is a deep reservoir of hatred and a ferocious need to punish. Where this reservoir of hatred and need to punish come from is anyone's guess. No one can explain the "why" of it. Maybe authoritarians were born that way. Maybe evil exists. Maybe authoritarians were wounded themselves and are passing that blight along. What we can say for certain is that, throughout human history and as far into the future as we can see, we will have to deal with authoritarians and the harm they inflict.

This is what your clients who are victims of authoritarian contact have had to deal with: a spiteful, cruel person who punished them relentlessly. Your client's bullying brother, cruel grandmother, cynical pastor, explosive boss, oh-so-charming uncle, intrusive sister, sarcastic father, or violent mother has taken their toll on her. With your help, she may come to see for the first time why she had so many school troubles, why she felt "stupid" and unequipped to deal with life, or why she had to "divorce" her family of origin. All of this may become clear to her for the first time.

I think that what my respondents have to report will provide you with the best picture available of the true nature of the authoritarian personality. Let's begin by looking at what I'm calling the aggression cluster, the first of three clusters of authoritarian traits and qualities.

2

THE AGGRESSION CLUSTER

In whatever ways that the authoritarian personality is defined or conceptualized, when you ask real people if they've had to deal with an authoritarian and they reply that they have, what they will almost invariably describe is a situation where someone was mean to them. Just plain mean. That meanness defined the matter.

Why all that meanness? Because what emerges from my respondents' reports is that authoritarians are operating from a hate-and-punish agenda. They look to be filled with a deep reservoir of hatred and a powerful need to punish. What naturally and regularly flow from that hate-and-punish agenda are meanness and aggressiveness.

The aggressions can be overt and "big" or rather more restrained and quite "small." However, even if small, having to deal with such wounding all through childhood or at the hands of a mate makes them loom large. In my own daily life, I see medium-sized mean and aggressive authoritarian behaviors all the time. Just about every day, when my wife and I take our twin granddaughters to the library, there, at one table or another, is a parent tyrannizing his or her child.

Under the guise of helping with homework, these parents ridicule, bully, demean, scare, and threaten their children. They say things like, "Why can't you remember the simplest thing?" "Why are you acting so stupid?" and "What's the matter with you?" Furious, they press in and loom over their child, who invariably ends up sobbing. Then the sobbing is attacked: "Why are you making a scene in the library!" Next follows some threat or scare tactic: "If you don't stop crying this instant, just wait until we get home!"

These parents are just being mean.

This is a diverse northern California neighborhood and these parents come in all shapes, sizes, and colors. This is a cross-cultural horror. Indian mother, Latino father, Scandinavian mother, African-American father, Japanese mother, every culture is represented. Some of these interactions are worse than others, some feel more clearly damaging, but all of them are in the same family of cruelty. I see with my own two eyes what my respondents will report.

I also see the passive authoritarians, the ones who frown and furrow their brows but mind their hatred in public. To take one trivial but telling example, I intended to buy some potato chips from a vending machine in the library. I only had a five-dollar bill and I didn't quite trust the machine to return the correct change, so I went up to the desk and asked the librarian if she could change the five-dollar bill. I could see that she was conflicted. Her mean nature wanted her to say no. Her civilized veneer and job description obliged her to say yes. As a compromise, she said, "Yes, but only because I'm going to the bank today. The next time, I may not be going to the bank and I won't be able to change any money."

Producing a response of this sort makes no sense unless you understand the core authoritarian hate-and-punish agenda and likewise understand that millions of passive authoritarians restrain themselves in public and wreak their havoc in private (or in experiments that encourage them to punish). You can tell from one or two such interactions with a passive-aggressive authoritarian that he or she is someone who is going to have profound negative consequences on anybody who remains in prolonged contact with him or her.

The aggressiveness I'm describing in this chapter is not restricted to beatings or destroyed furniture. It can look and sound very quiet; but it comes from that same hate-and-punish place and over time does its certain damage. Your client who has been affected by authoritarian wounding may not have large-sized aggressions to report but rather an ominous, scary childhood universe or a strangulating, rule-bound one. However different these stories, what you will see as a family resemblance is the meanness present.

In future chapters, we'll examine two other clusters: an exploitation cluster and a narcissism cluster. Ultimately, it's hard to decide what is most fundamentally true about an authoritarian, that he or she is primarily mean, exploitative, or narcissistic. All three are present and all three are important. Let's begin by focusing our lens on the 12 traits or qualities that make up the aggression cluster.

Hatred and Anger

A central truth about an authoritarian is that he or she is coming from a place of hatred. As respondent Max put it,

> My father hated just about everything. His hatred was very different from anger or resentment or even rage. It wasn't an emotion, really, but a position, an attitude toward life. Anything could be hated, including things that he'd claimed to love and admire just the second before. You could fall from grace in a split second because he was so ready to hate—it was like hatred was always right there on the tip of his tongue.

Cruelty

Cruelty naturally flows from hatred. We shake our heads at the barbarisms of fascism or the barbarism of parents who made it into the news for torturing their children, but the fact of the matter is that, given the sheer number of authoritarians among us, in most families someone is regularly being treated cruelly. One of the long-lasting effects of this cruelty is deep confusion on the victim's part, as he or she tries to make sense of what he or she did to deserve all that cruel treatment and what made him or her so unlovable. How often must these thoughts and feelings be contributing to the despair, anxiety, or chaos your client is presenting? Just asking the simple question, "Were you treated cruelly as a child?" or "Did you feel unloved as a child?" can get the conversation started.

Punishment

Because they are full of hatred, authoritarians need to punish others. They are likely to advocate for capital punishment, for harsh punishment for all offenders, and to angle for punishment obliquely, for example, by adopting a "right to life" position so as to punish women for getting pregnant. They are always alert for an opportunity to punish someone, especially family members. As respondent Mary explained, "My mother had an authoritarian personality, was angry all the time, and exploded just about every day. One time I fell off a swing and broke my ankle—and got beaten for crying. That's who she was."

Violence, Aggression, and Assaultive Behavior

Authoritarians are regularly assaultive and violent and even more often – sometimes constantly – in a state of barely suppressed near-violence. Here's how respondent Cynthia put it:

> My grandmother nearly killed my mother when she was sixteen, at which point my grandfather removed my mom from the home and put her in a halfway house. My mother became pregnant with me at age nineteen and grandmother successfully lobbied to get her committed in order to take over guardianship of me. She continually called me a whore, a slut, and a good-for-nothing, and told me that I would never amount to anything. I was removed from the home at age sixteen after my grandmother beat me with her cane and broke my collarbone for having a boyfriend.

Threats and Scare Tactics

Authoritarians want their victims to fear them. Respondent Robert explained,

> I was married to an authoritarian woman. I always felt afraid of her in little and big ways. I quickly learned that she slept with a gun under her pillow and on numerous occasions she threatened to kill me if I didn't do something she wanted

me to do. We fought constantly and she would always win because she was willing to 'go for the jugular' and hurt me. My self-esteem went down the toilet, I felt ashamed for being bullied by her, and ashamed of myself for not leaving.

Rigidity and Obsession with Control

The authoritarian's aggressive need to control is regularly the first attribute to which respondents point. In a characteristic response, Barbara explained about a previous boyfriend,

> When he spoke about his relationship expectations, they were presented as rules, givens, and truths that ought to be obvious to anyone. These included what I could and couldn't say to friends and family (for example, I was not allowed to express concerns about the relationship, because that equaled disloyalty). In order to monitor my compliance, he bugged our phone and put spyware on the household computer. When he 'caught' me (via the bugged phone) asking a friend for advice about one of his behaviors, he responded by throwing my belongings into giant trash bags and insisting that I choose, right there on the spot, a destination for myself and 'all of my crap.'

Destructiveness

One way to punish is to destroy. Authoritarians are destructive – toward individuals, toward whole groups, and toward objects, too. As respondent Bill explained,

> I was raised by an authoritarian father who could be loving at times but who also had an explosive rage. He never hit us but he destroyed objects like the television and the headboards of beds and front doors. His rages were terrifying and my mother never stood up to him and didn't realize how sick he really was because he had a very fancy job, high up in the New York City business world. If we questioned him, we were screamed at or ridiculed. He was interested in sleeping

around with women and making sure we looked good—and when he didn't get his way he destroyed things.

Readiness and Impulsivity

Authoritarians, even when they aren't acting overtly aggressive, are on a short inner leash and often do not need much provocation to explode, to act cruelly, or to punish. This fact helps explain why "regular people" are so quick to mete out extreme punishment in experimental settings. A huge number of "regular people" are authoritarians just waiting to show their true colors. Since they are so ready, they are also frequently highly impulsive: like a simmering kettle that suddenly whistles shrilly, authoritarians will "suddenly" and out of the blue aggress. Their impulsive aggression – that belt to the child, that bit of ridicule, that racial slur – only looks to be out of the blue – in fact, such behaviors are easy to understand, given all that simmering readiness. This reality has many implications for the therapeutic relationship: for one, your client, who had to deal with all this readiness and impulsivity, may be walking on eggshells in session because he or she doesn't really trust anyone not to suddenly turn dangerous.

Low Agreeableness

Agreeableness is a technical term in psychology, one of the Big Five personality traits first described by Allport, Odbert, and Cattell. In the literature, low agreeableness has been associated with selfishness, narcissism, antisocial tendencies, poor social adjustment, impatience, inflexibility, harshness, and an unforgiving nature. Authoritarians, whether overtly aggressive or publicly passive, love to not agree – to dispute, to quarrel, to deride, to ridicule, to just say no – because not agreeing creates grievances that then lead to opportunities for punishment. You say something, the authoritarian in your life says "No!" in some attacking way, you try to stick to your guns, a battle ensues, and one way or another you end up getting punished. From a hate-and-punish perspective, hardly anything serves your needs better than invariably not agreeing and turning every possible interaction into a war that allows you to brandish your weapons.

Domination

The three cluster traits of aggression, exploitation, and narcissism come together in an authoritarian's need to dominate. He or she will dominate wherever it feels safe to dominate or wherever his or her hatred is greatest. This produces what can look like a paradox: one authoritarian will bully the weakest child in the family; another authoritarian will butt heads with the strongest child. What we are witnessing is not a paradox but the fact that the first authoritarian is choosing his or her easiest, safest target, whereas the second authoritarian, full of rage at his or her stubborn child's rebellion, feels compelled to win that war. Sometimes an authoritarian will choose to try to dominate an easy target and sometimes a hard target – say, if you are Hitler, Poland versus the United States. In either case, he or she is coming from the same hate-and-punish place.

Sadism

If you are filled with hatred and a deep need to punish, and if you get the chance or make the chance to punish, inflict harm, and hurt someone, you get some release and a feeling that we might as well call pleasure. That's sadism in a nutshell. The smile of pleasure that we associate with sadists may be the only genuine smile that an authoritarian gets to experience, as it is only when he or she is inflicting pain and brutally punishing someone that the hatred has an outlet. Because of an authoritarian's exploitative nature and preoccupation with sex, this dynamic often plays itself out as sexual sadism, but it is by no means limited to sexual sadism. Any sadism will do.

Quixotic, Unclear Rules

Authoritarians, who may or may not have any personal interest in abiding by rules, love rules for other people. The more quixotic and unclear the rules, the better, as quixotic, unclear rules are the least possible to follow. Such rules are inevitably broken, opening the door to punishment for the rule-breaker. For an authoritarian, the rules are there *to be broken*, so that punishment can follow. This dynamic helps to explain why an authoritarian is so often irritated to the point of violence when a rule is *followed*, since he was hoping for a violation and an opportunity for punishment. Likewise, this helps explain why a child can never get the praise he or she was hoping to receive for following the authoritarian's rules: following them doesn't please him, it upsets him!

Authoritarians are consistently themselves. That doesn't mean that they are always punishing, ridiculing, yelling, destroying or "looking authoritarian." Rather, it means that there is a consistent logic to their behaviors and completely understandable why they might be cynically charming one moment, aggressively tyrannical the next, passive and cowardly the next, and so on. As respondent Paul put it,

> My dad could be sitting quietly reading the newspaper – and still you knew exactly who he was and exactly what he was capable of. It didn't matter if he happened to be patting the dog or whistling a tune – all that was needed for him to turn terrible was some stray thought passing through his head. He didn't need provocation, though he was always looking for provocation; he didn't need anything. He was a tyrant through and through – weak, sadistic, miserable – whether he was screaming or singing a show tune.

As we begin to understand an authoritarian's underlying hate-and-punish agenda, which, when married with narcissism and a need to exploit others, manifests as sadism, destructiveness, manipulation, and all the rest, we get a clearer picture of what an authoritarian is "really doing" when, for example, he or she creates rules that are impossible to understand and impossible to follow. Rules become an instrument of aggression, which, for an authoritarian, is their real purpose. Let's look at this phenomenon a little more closely, as it isn't very well known and yet wreaks havoc in the lives of your clients (and will almost certainly play itself out in session).

3

PLEASE BREAK MY RULES!

Some examples of authoritarian aggression, like beatings, are obvious enough as instances of aggression and as traumatic events. But some examples of authoritarian aggression – for example, the ways in which the rules an authoritarian lays down are used as weapons and as a means to punish – are less obviously aggressive and less clearly as traumatic as they are. Your clients who may not have been the victims of aggressions like beatings may still have been assaulted by the rules they had to live with or still have to live with and by the punishments meted out to them for breaking those rules.

This is significant in their lives and also significant to you as you work with them in session. It's important to remember that your clients who have been harmed by authoritarian contact have been aggressed against, regularly and repeatedly punished, and may come to session expecting to be punished and fearing aggression from you. Holding these expectations and fearful in this way, they are likely primed to see your words, gestures, body positioning, and interventions through that lens.

They may react with passive submission, making you think that they agree with your comments or proposals, they may be quick to counterattack, they may announce that you feel intimidating and that being in your presence feels dangerous. This is all natural, given that they have been repeatedly punished for no good reason.

Authoritarians punish not for "good reasons" but because a need to punish "the other" is a key driving force in their motivational makeup. A defining characteristic of an authoritarian is that he wants "the other" punished. If he or "someone like him" is guilty of something, he wants that person let off the hook. When, however, he designates someone as "the other," he wants that person or those people punished roundly and thoroughly.

If you know who a given authoritarian holds as the other, you know a lot about him and you can predict with great accuracy his opinions, his policies, his agenda, and his hit list. He may, for example, hold "men" as like him, and whatever men do as acceptable, and hold "women" as the other, and hate everything they do. A given authoritarian may, for example, designate his son as golden and incapable of doing any wrong and his daughter as pathetic and incapable of doing anything right. The son is never punished and the daughter is always punished. The first becomes yet another narcissist, and the other is now sitting across from you in session.

What look like huge inconsistencies, contradictions, or paradoxes in a given authoritarian's way of being vanish when you understand how much of his behavior is coming from this need to punish. For instance, it seems inconsistent that a believer would believe that all of his sins can be washed away at the last minute just by announcing his faith while at the same believing that someone else, who presumably has exactly the same opportunity at heaven, is undoubtedly going to hell and deserves to go to hell. Why doesn't that other person have the same chance that he does? In what sense can the other be condemned by and for his actions if the authoritarian can rid himself of his sins at the very last minute?

There is nothing contradictory or paradoxical here. The authoritarian is simply positing a God in his own image. He sees God as on the side of people like him and against people not like him. The authoritarian will get off the hook; others can't be allowed off the hook. This hangs together perfectly. Is an authoritarian aware that he always lets people like himself off the hook and always wants "the other" roundly punished? Whether or not he knows, whether or not he experiences any cognitive dissonance, whether or not he feels like a hypocrite, he is nevertheless perfectly consistent in his position.

This basic consistency leads to the following dynamic. An authoritarian must maintain arbitrary, easy-to-change, hard-to-understand rules, rules that aren't really rules at all but rather a means of punishment. An authoritarian doesn't much care if he or those like him follow "the rules" but he is very vigilant about whether "the other" does or doesn't. Indeed, to the extent that "the other" does follow his rules, that irritates him, upsets him, and is essentially unacceptable, as this stymies his ability to punish. Accordingly, he changes the rules, modifies them, switches them – in that way "the other" is now suddenly in violation of "the rules."

The extent to which trying to abide by an authoritarian's rules irritates and upsets him, rather than pleases him, is a little-known part of the authoritarian puzzle. Trying to follow the sometimes strict, sometimes loose, always punitive and arbitrary rules laid down by an authoritarian is painful and difficult enough. When those rules are also selectively and hypocritically applied, that adds more pain. And when those rules aren't really rules at all, but rather, the means to an end, existing not because of some underlying value or principle but in order to justify punishment, that adds an especially toxic element to the situation.

Authoritarians, who may or may not have any personal interest in abiding by rules, love rules for other people. The more quixotic and unclear the rules, the better, since quixotic, unclear rules are the least possible to follow. Such rules are inevitably broken, opening the door to punishment for the rule-breaker. For an authoritarian, the rules are there *to be broken*, so that punishment can follow. This dynamic helps to explain why an authoritarian is so often irritated to the point of violence when a rule is *followed*, since he was hoping for a violation and an opportunity for punishment.

Likewise, this helps explain why the child or mate of an authoritarian can never get the praise he or she was hoping to receive for following an authoritarian's rules. Following them doesn't please him, it upsets him. This is another reason why close contact with an authoritarian is so wounding. When a child tries his or her best to follow the rules and is not only not rewarded for those efforts but instead is mocked, ridiculed, or in some other way demeaned, he or she grows smaller, weaker, and less competent.

Respondent Alice explained:

> My father-in-law was an extreme authoritarian. Everyone in his family tried to live by his rules, because punishment was severe if you violated them. Breaking the rules cost you a volatile verbal assault followed by days of silence and a cold shoulder. I was subjected to this after I married into the family and the longer I stayed married to his son, the more I was treated as a natural, real daughter, which you may guess was not a bargain.
>
> Once everyone finally learned the current rules so as to keep peace with him, he changed them to something else without notifying anyone. No one ever knew what we had done wrong when the volcano exploded and the silent treatment fell. My sister-in-law and my husband and numerous others in the extended family were exiled for periods of time, varying from a few days to years, and no one ever knew exactly what it was that had touched the expulsion off. In fact, after a time, it seemed as if someone ALWAYS needed to be in the penalty box with my father-in-law.
>
> It was very hurtful in numerous ways, and the older my spouse becomes, the more prone he is to re-enact these behaviors with his loved ones and friends, especially after his father passed away eight years ago and he no longer has the reminder of what it feels like to be on the receiving end. I clearly do not understand it. I cannot imagine the payoff. I cannot imagine that it's more satisfying to be continually right than being loved. It is a very hurtful legacy that this man has left for those behind.

The reservoir of hatred that is one of an authoritarian's most salient characteristics requires that an authoritarian find ways to exact punishment. He needs to find fault almost more than he needs to breathe. To make sure that you are regularly at fault, he changes the rules. This dynamic addles the victim's mind. Especially if she is a child, she is bound to wonder why she can't do a better job of following the rules, why her objectively small errors or missteps produce such huge reactions and such severe punishment, and why she is the object of so little love and so much hatred.

Respondent Dolores explained:

I grew up with an authoritarian father. The relationship haunted me for years, well into my adulthood. Now, as someone mature at least in years, I can look back with some sympathy towards the twenty-something person that was my dad when I was little. He must have been miserable in his failing business and the rocky relationship he had with his own father.

I always knew in some way that he took his frustrations out on his family, but I must admit, I had never considered the possibility that he relished administering punishment. That is such a disturbing thought; and yet, when I consider it, I can see that he had a sadistic streak. I can think of several examples, but I will stick with one. For a number of years his favorite tool for discipline was a thin, rough cut, black stick of plastic with sharp edges, about two-and-a-half feet long, that he nicknamed, 'the Shillelagh.'

When threatening us, he used to slice this thing through the air and it made whooshing sound that simply terrified everyone in the household. And he was always threatening us, because we were always breaking one rule or another. I don't remember 'the rules' being laid out in any consistent way and I was often completely unaware of them until I violated one of them and suffered the consequences. A lot of times it felt like the rules were made up as we went along, like some type of perverse game where my dad as the rule-maker would always have control over us to do whatever he wanted to.

My father could be so charming and loving and then turn in an instant into the cruelest person you've ever met. You just never knew which personality you were going to be dealing with or what would set him off. Living with that kind of uncertainty as a small child felt soul-crushing. And the results were drastic and dramatically negative. You don't just walk away from that experience unscarred.

An authoritarian I knew operated in the following way. He ate whatever he wanted to eat and weighed a good hundred pounds too much. Under the guise of "creating healthy children," he made up preposterous eating rules for his children: for instance, that they could have exactly two potato chips each while he sat there eating a whole bag himself. His wife smiled at this; no one dared say "This is unfair" or "This is preposterous" or "You're a complete hypocrite."

Eating three potato chips got you a beating. But, since the beating was the goal, eating one potato chip also got you a beating. Getting potato chip crumbs on the rug got you a beating. Even accidentally breaking your potato chips got you a beating, all under the guise of "teaching good habits" and "not spoiling the kids." And if you managed to eat your two potato chips perfectly, *that* would infuriate him, since you'd ruined his opportunity to punish you. There was no way to successfully eat those two potato chips, which is why his children hated those potato chips. They were no treat – they were anything but.

Some authoritarians really do care about the exact nature of their rules, either because rulemaking and rule adhering are among the ways they are dealing with anxiety or because some important principle, value, or belief is at stake. The same need to manage anxiety that explains classic obsessive-compulsive behaviors like obsessive handwashing can explain some of an authoritarian's rule-connected behaviors. And a real belief may be at play: for instance, the belief that there is a God who cares a lot about whether you mix meat with dairy. These three different "reasons for rules" – as opportunity for punishment, as anxiety management, and as expression of belief – can and do exist in one-and-the-same person.

One rule may exist to manage anxiety, while a second may exist because it flows from a powerful belief, and a third may exist as an opportunity to punish. This helps to confuse an authoritarian's victims even more. Unaware of this dynamic, they must stand mystified as they experience some rules as ironclad and others as changeable, whimsical, and hypocritical. If, for example, your father truly believes that there is a God who will be infuriated if you eat meat and dairy at the same meal, it makes a kind of sense that he will fly off the handle at the sight of your roast beef-and-cheddar sandwich. But what about his hatred of the fact that you have a boyfriend when he has affairs all the time? That will just feel like hypocrisy and an excuse to punish you.

Part of the process of healing your client's authoritarian wound involves him or her coming to understand that he or she had no chance of getting it right vis-à-vis the authoritarian's rules. It was never the case that following the rules better or toeing the mark better was going to spare punishment or win approval. Your client had no chance. And if your client is still dealing with an authoritarian, he or she will want to look at the matter of rules in this new light.

I've spent a chapter on rules as a means to punishment because they are a less obvious feature of authoritarian aggression than bullying and beating and therefore less well understood as a source of trauma. I've also spent time on them because they affect what happens in session. What can you expect in session because of this dynamic? Any of the following and more:

- A given client may be very concerned that he or she understand the rules of therapy – what he or she can expect from you, what you expect from him or her – and if you don't have rules in place or don't particularly believe in rules, that may so upset your client that he or she won't want to continue with you.
- A given client may be very vigilant about consistency and be more concerned than you are about ending on the hour, more concerned than you are about never going over by even a minute, more upset than you think he or she ought to be if you go over with another client and keep him or her waiting, and quick to call you on any change or inconsistency, including changes which seem to have nothing to do with rules, like the arrangement of the furniture.

- All victims of authoritarian wounding stand in complicated relationship to the issue of rules. They are likely to prove ambivalent about rules, both wanting clear ones while upset at their essential arbitrariness, and highly sensitive to any perceived "violations" of the rules.

One feature of the aggression cluster is how authoritarians use rules as weapons. Another little understood feature of the aggression cluster is the way in which authoritarians tyrannize their victims even when the authoritarian in question is not aggressing, but only "standing ready" to explode. This readiness to explode forces victims to walk on eggshells in an effort, always futile, to prevent such an explosion. This dynamic is important for you to understand because, like the "rules" dynamic, it plays itself out in session, where your client may be "walking on eggshells" just as he or she did in her childhood home or does in his or her current home. We look at this dynamic next.

4

WALKING ON EGGSHELLS

Authoritarians also aggress by standing ready to aggress. Just as it is an act of aggression for your neighboring country to mass military at your border or to engage in military maneuvers in a threatening manner, it is an act of aggression when the authoritarian in your client's life barely suppresses his rage, makes a threatening gesture without delivering a blow, or "gets that look" that your client knows prefigures an explosion some percentage of the time. Actual aggression is scary and causes you to walk on eggshells, but the threat of aggression is also scary and leads to a similar outcome.

Authoritarians know this. The fellow in the bar who is always ready for a fight knows that he is giving off that vibe. Authoritarians, who love to dominate, who need to appear strong and forceful, know how to look aggressive and "just plain mean" without throwing a punch or destroying a chair. Just as we know to cross to street when someone scary is approaching, authoritarians know how to look like the scary one approaching. A readiness to aggress is a real feature of the aggression cluster and important for you as a helper to understand. Your client who has been victimized by an authoritarian may walk on eggshells with you, too, even though you are doing nothing in the least bit aggressive.

One of the many consequences your victimized clients can expect from authoritarian contact and authoritarian wounding is a lifelong heightened sense of vigilance, nervousness, worry, and anxiety. If they grew up with someone who was always ready to explode, always percolating meanness, always getting his belt or his barbs ready, that readiness to attack is likely to have permanently harmed them and negatively affected how they deal with everyone, you included. In his or her shoes, wouldn't you be cautious, suspicious, quick to recoil, and more rather than less defensive?

An authoritarian harms people not just by what he says and does, but by his readiness to speak and act in an authoritarian way. We sense this readiness, and it creates stress in us. Over time, this stress is wearing and even debilitating. We stay on edge because we just never know when the explosion may come, when the attack may commence, or when the meanness will erupt. Staying on edge in this way weakens us, opens us up to sickness, and demoralizes us. It is a powerful stressor and amounts to chronic stress.

We know that the aggressive behavior is coming because we sense that it is a deep-dwelling feature of the authoritarian's personality and connected to his or her hate-and-punish agenda. We don't need to see any particular behavior very often to know that the behavior is lurking there in the shadows. Theodor Adorno, in the classic *The Authoritarian Personality*, underlines this distinction between any particular overt behavior and the personality that generates the behavior. Adorno explained:

> According to the theory that has guided the present research, personality is a more or less enduring organization of forces within the individual. These persisting forces of personality help to determine responses in various situations, and it is thus largely to them that consistency of behavior – whether verbal or physical – is attributable. But behavior, however consistent, is not the same thing as personality; personality lies behind behavior and within the individual.
>
> The forces of personality are not responses but rather readinesses for response. Whether or not a readiness will issue in overt expression depends not only upon the situation of the moment but upon what other readinesses stand in opposition to it. It may be emphasized again that personality is mainly a potential; it is a readiness for behavior rather than

behavior itself; although it consists in dispositions to behave in certain ways, the behavior that actually occurs will always depend upon the objective situation.

Your authoritarian father, who is ready to explode, may not explode because you have company over for dinner, because he just exploded the moment before and released some venom, because he is being watched by someone in a position of authority and knows better than to explode, because someone stronger than him is in the room, or for some other reason. He is still that cruel tyrant who bullies and explodes – and everyone who knows him knows that. He just happens not to be exploding or bullying at that split second. The readiness is there but for the moment at least, no explosion.

Because an authoritarian stands ready to explode, ready to punish, and ready to otherwise aggress, everyone under his thumb tiptoes around, getting weaker and sicker in the process. What does a person do when she knows that the authoritarian in her life is always ready to speak and act like an authoritarian? She flinches. She keeps her distance. She makes wide circles. She keeps her mouth shut. Sometimes, to make sure that she isn't wrong in her assessment and unfairly judging the authoritarian, she tests him by saying something provocative or by breaking a cardinal rule – which of course provokes the authoritarian's wrath. As a result of her experiment she goes back into hiding, not testing those waters again very soon.

You can see how this dynamic might play itself out in session. A client might miss an appointment just to see if you will turn mean and reveal your true colors. He or she might intently watch you in ways that make you feel uncomfortable because he or she has learned to be highly vigilant in all power-and-authority situations. He or she might take your mild interventions more defensively than other clients do or remain stoically closemouthed. Even though you may have never aggressed against this client in any way, he or she is quite likely waiting to see if you will – and suspecting that you will.

Respondents to my Authoritarian Wound Questionnaire reported many varied examples of this authoritarian readiness. One respondent, Linda, reported that she spent her whole childhood walking on eggshells. It would have been hard to convince anyone outside of the family that her father was an authoritarian because he said so little, kept to himself, and was never physically violent. But inside the family, you just knew that he was a ticking time bomb. As far as she could remember, he only exploded a handful of times. But at those times, he turned into what she could only characterize as a monster. Those few monstrous moments so frightened the family that everyone remained permanently meek.

Another respondent, Adele, explained that she felt that she had been continually holding her breath throughout her childhood. She had no doubt but that this either contributed to or actually caused her severe asthma, made her a vigilant "control freak" with her own children, and produced her periodic migraines and dizziness. To this day, she still caught herself holding her breath and explained, "I have to remember to exhale. Half the time I feel like I'm not breathing at all!"

One characteristic outcome of this eggshell-walking is that victims are likely to experience more anxiety than the next person. Another characteristic outcome is that they are likely to feel incompetent and "stupid." Because one feature of anxiety is confusion, and because an authoritarian's constant readiness to attack produces constant anxiety in his victims, victims are likely to experience life as a state of constant confusion. There is a direct link between an authoritarian's readiness to harm and his children's school failures and life failures. If you're constantly anxious and confused, how smart will you feel and how competently will you perform?

To take one example of this dynamic, respondent Joanne noticed the following about herself. As she stood on the checkout line after doing her shopping, she would dissociate and feel herself floating away. Therefore, she was never prepared to pay when it was her turn in line. She always found herself fumbling around in her purse for her money or her credit card. She knew that she was infuriating the people in line behind her, who had to be thinking, "Doesn't that stupid woman know that she is going to have to pay?" In her 50s now, she realized that this had been going on forever: that her permanent anxiety had caused her to look stupid and feel stupid.

This "feeling stupid" will play itself out in session. A client who has always felt stupid is likely to feel incompetent in session, unable to come up with answers to the questions you pose, certain that he or she is not smart enough to deal with psychological material, and maybe even unaware of his or her inner life, having lived walled off from self-awareness. Your client may shake his or her head a lot, smile that self-deprecating smile that means "I'm not equal to what you're asking of me," and not prove a great help – at least in the beginning of your work together – at envisioning or cocreating solutions to the problems that get identified.

There is a straight line between growing up with an authoritarian and feeling stupid. There is a straight line between growing up with an authoritarian and feeling scared all the time. Even if the authoritarian in your life was actively bullying, violent, shaming, or cruel only some portion of the time, you grew up knowing that he or she was *still* an authoritarian even when quiescent. That awareness is almost certainly still built into you as heightened anxiety. That anxiety may show its face in any of the ways that anxiety manifests, from confusion to stomachaches to panic attacks to phobias. You walked on eggshells back then; quite likely you are still walking on them now.

It may also be the case that the authoritarian in your client's life never acted like an authoritarian until something triggered his or her true nature. This is a second, related sense of "authoritarian readiness." Just as the neighborhood butcher or lawyer may not show his or her authoritarian personality in public until a fascist comes to power, the authoritarian in your client's life may not access that well of hatred and may not start to punish until circumstances turn that potentiality into overt behavior.

For example, your client's mate may only begin to manifest his or her authoritarian nature when their first child arrives or when their first stubborn, rebellious child arrives. Maybe the proto-authoritarian fawned over the first child, who was pliant and docile, and as a result looked anything but authoritarian in his or her dealings with the family. Then the wilder child arrived ... and the beatings begin.

Likewise, an authoritarian's true colors may only emerge when his or her mate takes a stand and demands fair treatment. One respondent explained that so long as she was the meek wife her culture demanded that she be, her husband acted coldly but kindly enough toward her, making small concessions, allowing her some cultural "stretches" in terms of what she could wear and how she could behave, and in other ways acting "better" than many of her friends' husbands.

At a certain point after her three children were born, she decided that she wanted to enter the world of work. This her husband would not permit. She acquiesced and despaired, this capitulation creating a false harmony, until she could no longer tolerate her situation. The more she pressed, the more aggressive he became. The authoritarian that he always "could have been" and that her general acquiescence had kept at bay now appeared. Buttressed by his culture's acceptance of his patriarchal position and knowing that his actions would be sanctioned by his peers, he felt sure that he could safely aggress. He became violent toward her and violent toward their children.

This began her long journey out of her marriage and out of her culture. The more she asserted herself, the more aggressive her husband became. The violence escalated; the threats escalated; she and her children became increasingly endangered. What surprised her was that this didn't surprise her. She hadn't consciously known that her husband would be capable of such aggression and yet when it commenced and escalated she could only nod her head. She knew that it was coming from exactly the same person that she had married, a man who had appeared benign enough until circumstances ignited his authoritarian nature.

Many of your clients may have similar experiences, and these experiences are likely to remain unvoiced unless you ask about them. There are a variety of questions you can ask that get at this feature of your client's history. A simple one to ask is, "Did you feel frightened of someone in your childhood, even if you couldn't quite say why you felt frightened?" A second is, "You say that your father only exploded a few times. But were you always worried about him exploding?" In these and other ways you can begin to address the matter of "authoritarian readiness" in the lives of your clients.

With your help, your clients may begin to better understand the extent to which they are reacting to people and interacting with people as if they were all prospective authoritarians. Reacting in such ways may not be a completely bad policy, given how many authoritarians are out there and how many of them do not show their true colors at first blush. But it would be good if your clients gained insight into this dynamic, since their problems with trust can likely be traced back to the way in which they were obliged to walk on eggshells.

The idea of "authoritarian readiness" is an important concept to remember. It helps explain why everyday bakers, accountants, and homemakers can turn fascist so easily when a fascist leader comes forward. It helps explain why a given authoritarian may not "turn authoritarian" until circumstances, like a suddenly rebellious mate or the birth of a stubborn child, provoke him or her into behaving cruelly. And it helps explain why your clients who endured authoritarian wounding may have been so very deeply wounded, even though they were overtly aggressed against only infrequently.

5
I. HATE. MY. MOTHER.

The questions that respondents addressed when they took the Authoritarian Wound Questionnaire (see Appendix) walked them through a way of thinking about the authoritarian in their life and offered them the chance to consider certain distinctions: for instance, whether they experienced the authoritarian as more of an authoritarian follower or an authoritarian leader, whether the authoritarian, if it was the respondent's mother or father, had an "authoritarian parenting style" or was authoritarian "through and through," etc. Their reports provide a wonderful picture of how authoritarian contact wounds and what victims endeavor to do to heal and recover.

I'll present some of these reports as examples of the aggression cluster, some as examples of the exploitation cluster, some as examples of the narcissism cluster, and others in various contexts: for instance, in the context of the issues clients bring to session and the issues of working with victims in session. But each report does more than provide an example of one of these themes. Each report paints a picture of what harm looks like. I'm presenting them with minimal editing, in the respondent's own voice, so you can better understand what your clients may have experienced. If these reports speak to you, as I think they will, you might want to rethink how you take clients' history and perhaps afford your clients the opportunity to report in similar ways.

The first of these reports is Karen's. You will see many of the characteristic qualities of the authoritarian personality in Karen's mother: bigotry and prejudice, deceit, violence, religious cover, shaming behaviors, intrusiveness, an overwhelming hatred and need to punish, and more. You will also see that Karen's siblings do not concur with Karen's version of their childhood, leaving

Karen further perplexed, isolated, and alone. Remember that as victims of authoritarian contact, your clients may also be dealing with a deep wonder as to whether they really experienced what they believe they experienced – and, if they did experience all that, why the people around them are reporting such different experiences. Here is Karen's story.

* *

My mother is an exceptionally authoritative personality and it was hard for me growing up… and it's still hard. I am almost 60 years old, live 2,000 miles away from my mother (no accident), have a husband and three kids, yet it has been the most difficult, influential relationship in my life. She was and is a piece of work.

She made me wary and too worried about pleasing. I'm in first grade. I'm practicing the alphabet on that horizontal paper with the fat lines. I have trouble with a capital S. I erase it and try again. Still doesn't look right. I erase more. There's a hole in the paper now. I go to the bathroom and start to cry in the stall. I'm crying so hard I throw up. The teacher comes in and wants to know what the problem is. My paper, I tell her. I've made a hole. I'll probably make a "C" now. Years later, I find my report card from Grade 1. I always had straight A's. I am disheartened to read the comment from the teacher: "Karen tries too hard to please others."

When I was in second or third grade, my mother gave me a diary. She explained that it was for my private thoughts. At one point, I wrote in huge letters – one word to a page – I. HATE. MY. MOTHER!!! One day I got off the bus from school and walked in the house. I knew something was "off" as soon as I walked in. I always had my antennae up, and I could smell her "crazy" even though she did not drink and was not an alcoholic. She had read the diary. I was the worst daughter on earth. Worst in the family. And what I had done was wrong. *The Bible says, Honor Your Father and Mother. Where was the honor.* I was beaten with a belt.

I don't know if it was that time or another time, but I had to stand in the center of the family room and wait for my father to come home. My arms were outstretched in both directions, and she put a heavy book on each arm. I couldn't keep my arms straight and the books kept falling down because I was too small to handle the weight. She raged at me from a rocker in the corner of the room. *Pick. Up. The. Books.* She still had a belt in her hand. *No one wants you. You have no one,* she explained. *You'll be going to a Home for Wayward Girls. You're an ungrateful bitch. What did you think now?*

She never got an answer out of me. This happened again and again. My silence only infuriated her more. I knew she would hit me harder because of it, but the words just stuck in my throat. By the age of eight or nine I knew that if I screamed, it would just start another rampage. *Shut your shitty little mouth or I'll give you something to cry about.*

I am in fifth grade. I want hair like the other girls in my class, which is a big problem because the majority of them have blond, straight hair. Mine is dark and curly because my father is Italian. It doesn't look good no matter what I do. The style in the 1960s is parted in the middle, or two braids, or a ponytail with two wispy sideburns. I try two braids. I am sent to my room to get the braids out of my hair. I am never to wear braids because it will make my hair kinky like a black person's. She hates the sight of me. She screams at me literally every time I walk through the family room. And my stomach is too big – *suck it in! You look like you're pregnant* (I'm about ten.) She is angry when I get my period and constantly reminds me to get my filth out to the garbage can outside.

If there is some weird thing on TV about sex, or girls being raped, or any creepy thing, she calls me in to watch it with her. *Sit there and watch this.* I can't tell you how supremely uncomfortable these sessions would make me feel. And when it was over, she asks me, *Well, what do you think about that?* I shrug. I say "Nothing." The truth is, I don't know what to say. I don't know the right answer. I just want to disappear into the cellar. *A boy will say anything to get into your pants. He doesn't care about you. You're just like a dog he pisses on and then he's on to the next. Remember that.* I nod glumly and shuffle back to my room. I escape into books. Books saved me. *You may be book smart, Karen, but you are horse dumb.*

Home from school, walking in the back door. *You may think you are fooling me, but you are not fooling anyone.* I am wracking my brain trying to figure out where this is coming from. What have I done? It dawns on me – the ice skates. My dad had bought me a pair of Hyde skates – high quality beautiful white leather skates. She made him take them back to the store because they were too expensive, and I continued to wear a pair of black hand-me-down skates from my brothers. I loved ice skating. *I'm going to divorce your father* (they remain married), *and then, you know what? You will have no place to go. I know what you're trying to pull with your father* (um, that makes one of us), *and let me tell you, your father doesn't want you. I don't want you. I'm going to take your sister and move to North Carolina* (where she is from). *You will have no place to go.*

I am in high school. I've done well on the PSATs, enough so that I receive a letter from Harvard inviting me to apply. There's a meeting with local alumni. I want to go to the meeting. I want to apply to Harvard, just to see if I can get in, I tell her, not to go there. I know I'm going to UConn (and my parents have decided I'm going to be a business major because I'm not good enough at math to be an engineering major), because I have three older brothers, and I'm the fourth one to come through. She stops talking to me because of the Harvard issue. This goes on for weeks, maybe months. It becomes the undercurrent of the next few years. I remember I spoke up at the dinner table at one point, and she hit me so fast and so hard across the face with her hand and a dishcloth, I saw stars. I believe she truly hated the sight of me, she hated me down to my bones.

There's a high school orchestra recital. Despite being a poor violinist (I sit last chair with the second violins), I keep playing. I don't have private lessons. I don't practice (*Shut that door I can still hear you!*). Mainly it's a way to get out of the house. I don't even bother to tell my parents about the recital. I have the long black dress on – it's actually my mother's – and I love wearing it even though we aren't the same size. My mother was not buying me a separate black skirt and white blouse, and she didn't care what the conductor had to say about it. I am on my way out the door. I have put sprigs of baby's breath in my hair. I think I look pretty great. I'm hoping to see my friend's older brother there. *Where do you think you're going?* I explain about the concert. She wants to know why I didn't tell her about it. Because I didn't think you wanted to go. Something snaps in her. She picks up the black iron poker from the fireplace and tries to hit me over the shoulders and back. I'm faster, though, and I spin around with my arms up to protect myself.

How dare you raise a hand to me. She is raging and screeching – she is completely in another orbit. Who did I think I was? I wanted her to get a second mortgage on the house so I could show off and go to Harvard. *Well that isn't going to happen you conniving little bitch.* I was trying to seduce my father. I was disgusting. (Note that my dad barely spoke to me on any given day and dropped me off three blocks from school in the mornings because he was always running late.) *Well he doesn't love you. I'm going to divorce the son of a bitch. You will have nothing. You will have nowhere to live. I am going to sell this house.* I don't remember anything else about the night or if I ever made it to the concert.

Last year, I lost a cousin in a car accident in North Carolina. I hadn't seen my mother's side of the family in 40 years. My sister and I decided to attend. I knew my mother would no longer be flying back and I wanted to see if my memories of my maternal grandmother's house and other relatives compared to the real thing. An older female cousin picked me up from the airport, and we had a chance to share a long afternoon before my sister arrived. We were both looking for explanations. Her mother and my mother were sisters.

In her family of five, there were heavy casualties. A brother with suicidal tendencies, another brother dead (something related to his liver), a sister struggling with alcohol dealing with a daughter of her own who overdosed (big family secret – I was told she died of pneumonia); it was bad. My Aunt Wilma had favorites she liked to pick on. Her son Johnny refused to go to her funeral and still won't speak about her. One daughter decided not to have children for fear of continuing the line.

We talked about our other aunts (there were six) and ticked through the female offspring. They were all a mess. The common traits were astounding. These women were jealous of other women, angry all the time, could not empathize with anyone, could not show affection, and did not value anyone else's accomplishment. There was a high degree of loyalty to the Baptist church. There were long Wednesday services, long Sunday services, and other obligations like "picking beans for the pastor." And to hear my cousin talk, these churches survive today and there is high drama in every one of them – affairs, pedophilia, etc.

Some consequences I have noticed:

- Inability to make decisions (second-guessing and more second-guessing)
- Never able to articulate what I want, because I never seem to know (Should I stay in this job? Leave? What do I want to do instead?)
- Loss of self (I can't even answer the question, "What's your favorite song?")
- Too eager to please
- Too accepting of responsibility for others (from family to work responsibilities)
- Susceptible to criticism
- Lack of resilience
- Incapable of joy/prone to sadness
- Susceptible to guilt, shame
- Lack of boundaries
- No vocabulary to express self
- Anxious demeanor (waiting for the next bad thing to happen)
- Watchful, attuned to the states of mind of other people

I have been diagnosed with dysthymia and I do struggle with darker episodes from time to time. I take an antidepressant. I feel as though I was born under a cloud – even in my baby pictures I look worried. I think in a way I was robbed of the capacity to feel joy because of my mother. I am trying to undo the long-term effects. My intention is to continue to work toward uncovering what brings me happiness and solace. Talk to me next year!

By the way, my brothers do not share my recollections. They have papered over them for one reason or another, and they never experienced the side of her that I did. My sister had a different mother, too, really, by virtue of being born eight years after the first four kids. The effect, though, is that it is difficult to maintain the "truth" of my story when there are no collaborators and no witnesses. Of course, I know better than to expect some kind of grand moment with my mom where she owns up to what she did and how much she hurt me. But I have lost the urge to blame her or punish her, her health is failing, and I only wish her safe passage.

* *

For helpers: If you knew the above about a client of yours, how might it influence the way you went about helping him or her?

6

PERFECTION WAS THE MINIMUM

It would have been easy to provide story after story of violent authoritarian aggressiveness from the responses I received. But it's important for you as a helper to understand that your client may have been harmed by an aggressiveness that did not involve physical assault but that involved the aggressive use of rules, as I described previously, and by the aggressive use of standards, as you'll see in this chapter.

Aggression is not just slaps, spankings, and beatings. It can also manifest as quietly as being forced to continually act in conventional and acceptable ways or always being told that what you are doing isn't good enough. The following two stories illustrate this "quiet" face of authoritarian aggressiveness. First is Monica's story.

* *

I have dealt with an authoritarian personality in the person of my mother. There was tremendous love between us, and, for many years, enmeshment also. I didn't do any adolescent rebellion until my late 20s. I "did a geographic" repeatedly starting at age 15, always trying to see the world, the world beyond her boundaries, which she ruled, from my perspective, with an iron hand and a right way for everything. She was always astonished that I was not afraid to travel, but I loved figuring out the rules and roles in new places without reference to what she thought was correct. I learned to trust my intuition and feelings.

I think my mother was more of an authoritarian follower than a leader because she was always trying to avoid friction and make sure that everybody was happy. All my friends wanted her for their mother and all her students (she was a master teacher from kindergarten to third grade) worshipped her until her death.

That always confused me, but years of therapy helped me see that they loved her because she thought they were all bright and wonderful and she provided structure. Most of them joyfully lived up to her orderly standards and expectations, then went home to daily chaos.

I, on the other hand, had to live with her in a "just so" storybook life. For years I could not remember my dreams and figured out that I never was allowed to dawdle in that half-awake state where dreams are accessible. I woke up to her voice, like a gong, with my perfectly matched outfit laid out on the other twin bed: pastel, hand-smocked dress, matching panties, socks with lace trim, grosgrain hair ribbons. That was the role she had cast me in.

I used to think that she also wrote the script. I finally got angry when I noticed that she always ignored me as a child when I talked about something that I was very excited or passionate about, something that she did not comprehend or had not scripted. She loved to watch me saying trite, clichéd chitchat sorts of things: she loved me when I was her perfect "jewel of a child," as her friends liked to call me.

Much later, when I was in my 50s, my mother asked why she always had to hear about my projects and adventures (my travels, my work in independent film) from others. I told her that I had learned long ago that she was not interested in what interested me and I described how she used to talk right through me at the dinner table, just to ask for the salt. She sometimes said that she hated working with adults, because they would never just follow the rules and do what they were supposed to, unlike kids. For many years I thought that her rules for everything were commonly held. It took me a while to learn that this was her take on the world and how she managed her own fears.

The personal consequences of this wound were a lack of adult coping skills and severe depression, in spite of an Ivy League education and world travel. This made entering the world of work with its blatant racism and sexism hard to deal with. I would hide in my apartment when not at work and finally I decided to "get married instead of hospitalizing myself." After having my daughter, I had a surge of insight and energy, which took me to therapy in order not to give her "a crazy mama." Since then I've been doing well, had a couple of breakthroughs with my mother, but have continued to have monstrous writing blocks around major projects which is truly debilitating for someone who knew she was a writer at the age of 11.

I built up my skills over the years, but the writing block still stalks me. The bigger the project, the more monstrous the block. There is another consequence that I have become aware of only in the last year: my attachment style and my inability to sustain a relationship with a man. I have truly believed all my life that to give and accept love means that you have to be the part of yourself that the other loves and must give up the rest of yourself. I see now I avoid closeness because I see the choice between being myself in my full, cranky, creative wholeness or being loved by someone else.

A long time ago, I decided to grow up and keep growing, being myself. I'm thinking about returning to therapy to deal with this because, for the first time in my life, I feel lonely! I think this means that I have finally succeeded in getting my mother complex out of my head where she tried to crowd me out of my own mind. Now that I experience a new level of psychic autonomy, I am able to feel lonely. This is an achievement.

What helped? Therapy, workshops, and the serendipitous blessing of friends who really saw me and valued all my stuff that my mother didn't comprehend or welcome. Most significant was the birth of my daughter, which generated the courage to change and grow up without knowing where it would lead. With her I learned how to love another person and how to accept love.

I did not have a complete break with my mother. We maintained a positive connection, actually improving it after many years, but, except for 15 years, I maintained the geographical distance that I needed. For those 15 years, however, I lived next door to her. She was a great help with my daughter when I traveled and they adored each other. Then for two years I lived with her after I sold my house and decided which way to go: New York City or Los Angeles. One day we reenacted one of our age-old scenarios and I saw it in the moment! I had disagreed with her, and she was walking away, with tears in her eyes and her shoulders slumped, like "poor pitiful me." I recognized it and I spoke to it, normalizing the ability to disagree with those you love.

She was astonished! This was a revelation to her: that you could disagree and even get angry without destroying love! Those 15 years next door to her I was very conscious of living my life to my own specifications under her eyes: having men I was involved with in the house without hiding them, writing in my journal in front of her, wearing loud colors and wild hair. She was very literal and concrete. It had been a revelation to me that she thought "writing" meant penmanship (at which she was very good). As I sat writing faster than the speed of light in my journal she commented, "I could never write like that! Nobody would be able to read it." I laughed and said nobody was supposed to read it, that I was just spilling ideas, feelings, impressions, and images. She was even more astonished.

She had always acted as if she had no inner life and couldn't imagine that anyone else did either. When I was little, quietly imagining outrageous adventures or later, reading, she always acted like I was doing "nothing" and encouraged me to go out and play with the other kids. In therapy, I talked about how she seemed to think she had a right to stomp around in my head and re-arrange the furniture: to tell me what to think and how to feel. I am sure that my mother isn't the worst authoritarian in the world, not by a long shot, but that doesn't mean that her particular brand of controlling didn't harm me – and was uncalled for.

* *

In Sarah's story, which follows, her mother's repeated command, "Perfection is just the minimum, Sarah," is a perfect example of how a child can be diminished, traumatized, and harmed by the aggressive application of absurd standards. You do not have to beat a child to ruin a child. When you're investigating authoritarian wounding in session, keep an eye out for unfair, traumatic applications of standards in your client's life.

* *

Growing up with two authoritarian parents was emotionally stifling. I felt like there was something terribly wrong with me that I could never fix because it was simply "part of me," and that unless I could conquer it with no help and through being perfect at all times, I would never fit into society and never be able to take care of myself. That all my poor choices were caused because I am attention-seeking, outspoken, and willful, and that women are to be quiet, serene, soft-spoken, peacekeeping, modest, capable, caregiving, forgiving, and above all, perfect.

Any woman who claims she is experiencing "sexism" or "sexual harassment" has clearly, and above all, intentionally, brought it on herself by being attention-seeking, outspoken, and willful. In Dad's mind, there is no more sexism and racism in this country. It is gone. To claim you experience it is because you're "looking for someone to blame for your problems other than yourself."

Dad is an authoritarian leader. He thinks he is right, his belief system is The Belief System, and everyone else in the world who is not as successful or as good as him is that way due to their own personal failure. Dad is big on "personal responsibility," which to him means you never ask for help, you always do it right the first time, you make the same decisions he would make, you act with a magnanimous and serene countenance at all times, you never complain, you do not experience frustration, you feel joy even when treated miserably (because there is no mistreatment: only things you brought on yourself), you only ever succeed and you never brag about it, and you sit at his feet for guidance and wisdom (even about things in which you're an expert).

Dad is the personality (he is innately that way with family, friends, acquaintances, colleagues, superiors, and inferiors). Mom has an authoritarian parenting style (she adopted this mentality only where I was concerned; in all other aspects of her life she is collaborative and team-oriented). As a result, and because of the two of them equally, I have a total lack of trust in my own ability to care for myself, feeling all the way into my 40s that I am a failure for not being like my parents, always believing other people before myself (WAY too trusting of them) because I have been taught to believe that, since I am not like Dad's Ideal Female, I am seriously flawed and unable to function like a normal human.

I was taught that others have already/automatically earned your total respect and trust, no matter who they are, but that YOU (in my case, I) must start from the beginning to earn the trust and respect of those around you. Oh, and the starting point of earning trust and respect as a human being? Perfection. You are not worthy of respect, autonomy, companionship, employability, etc. unless you are PERFECT. And as Mom would repeatedly state, "Perfection is only the MINIMUM, Sarah."

I was severely bullied in school for being ugly (I was not a cute kid) and fat (I ate my feelings from age 5 through 13). I was punished for "allowing" it to happen. This included groundings, being sent to my room, lost privileges, and if I complained too much, spanking. I was specifically told after one particularly bad incident that "Kids don't just DO these things to other kids, Sarah. You must have done something to deserve it." Once, after being beaten up, I asked my parents to teach me to defend myself. They told me that I was to turn the other cheek and under NO circumstances was I to fight back or there would be consequences at home, too.

Also, I hate my name after having it said in anger and disgust so many times. I literally still wince every time I hear it. What has helped? Staying the hell away from them. Lots of self-help (psychological journals, studies, professional blogs, etc.) I can't do therapy because I have such a strong, unconscious desire to be perfect and to not have problems that I can neither trust nor be completely honest with a therapist. I feel completely judged and infantilized by the therapy process and will tell the therapist whatever he or she wants to hear just so I can be judged as "competent" or "normal" or "acceptable." So, I have learned about the various therapies, pathologies, and methodologies on my own... it is WAY easier to be honest with myself than with an "authority."

But I guess I do suggest that others try therapy. Help yourself, read a lot about your experience, and do try therapy... and don't quit after one therapist. If five or ten make you feel worse, you may have the same issues that I do. No matter, you must prioritize yourself: the variance in what is "normal" for humans is so wide and so great, that it is highly probable that your natural self, the one you would have been without the authoritarian poisoning your psyche, is an amazing person with unique, intelligent perspectives and wondrous ability. Go out and find and heal YOU. That inner voice that knows you are right about yourself, knows what is best for yourself, knows how to love and respect yourself, and knows the authoritarian is full of crap? Listen to that voice!

* *

7

WHOLE SCARRED FAMILIES

If your client has been wounded by an authoritarian, you can expect that other family members will have been wounded as well. If the authoritarian was your client's father or mother, you can expect that his or her siblings were also damaged. If the authoritarian is or was his or her mate, you can expect that their children have not escaped unscathed. The wounds of all of these various family members then affect your client.

In this chapter, I'll present two stories that illustrate how a victim of authoritarian wounding is often doubly wounded because of the scarring of other family members. In the following report, the suicide of Laura's brother, himself a victim of authoritarian wounding, becomes another trauma for her to endure. In working with victims of authoritarian contact, expect that they will manifest multiple wounds, since they are bound to be dealing with a whole damaged family. Here is Laura's story.

* *

My father was a tyrannical presence in my family home. We lived according to his emotions – if he didn't want to do something, we didn't do it, and if my mother pushed, he became very angry, petulant, withdrawn, etc., until it was just easier to do what he wanted.

One thing that I learned was that my feelings didn't matter. I remember once, at the age of six, being extremely angry at him for something, and him forcing me to tell him that I loved him. I remember how hard it was to shove the words out of my mouth, but I guess I knew that I didn't have a choice.

I was always on edge, too. I remember coming home from being away at sleepovers and the first thing I'd do was try to find my sister to ask her what sort of mood dad was in. I suppose this was so that I'd know whether or not I had to be on guard or try to avoid him. At the same time, I was his emotional caregiver. If the dinner conversation went in a direction he didn't like, he'd sometimes run off to his room and slam the door, and I was the one who always went after him and comforted him.

I remember that he'd tell me never to marry someone who wasn't as sensitive as I am. At other times, he'd pull out his shotgun and sit with it, passively threatening suicide – I suppose trying to make us pledge our undying love. When I was about 14 I stopped reacting to this (I was the baby, so by this point everyone else had given up as well). Eventually he stopped this extreme behavior – but I remember still feeling very guilty about no longer caring, but also like I'd been backed into a corner. It felt like the only way to survive was not to be manipulated by him anymore. This happened with all of us in our family, so as a result he turned to another woman who would give him what he wanted. My parents split up when I was 18.

I would say that my father was an authoritarian leader more than a follower. However, from what I know from his childhood, he was a follower as a kid. His own father was a twisted tyrant who would insist – I've heard from family stories – that his wife not wear underwear under her dresses so he could 'have her' whenever he wanted, including in front of the children. I think my father became a leader perhaps because he was so damaged as a kid and didn't want to ever be in that situation again. I don't know – but his tyrannical behavior and absolute insistence on getting his own way makes me define him as a 'leader' (and his new wife is now his follower).

Nor would I say that he had an 'authoritarian parenting style' – he was an authoritarian through and through. His authoritarianism hasn't ever wavered, and it comes out with his friends and other family members as well. For instance, he has some friends, a couple, one of whom is very ill, and they have asked him and his wife not to stop by late at night. Yet my father and his wife continue to show up after normal hours, sometimes as late as 11 p.m. at night.

I think that the following are among the consequences of growing up with an authoritarian dad. One is an overwhelming sense of guilt when I put my own needs first. A second is my inability to relate to my siblings without casting on them the same judgment my dad leveled on them. For example, my sister was adopted, and it was quite clear that my dad didn't really want her. He treated her differently – for instance, he drilled a peephole into her room from the basement and covertly sexually abused her in other ways. I've only realized in the past couple of years, since my brother died, and since my sister and I have both ended our relationship with our dad, that I cast judgments on her and subtle rejections that I'd picked up from him.

I also find it very hard to be vulnerable with my husband or to simply state my needs. I often misread his normal quietness as passive-aggressive anger. I've also struggled a lot with one of the effects of the corrosive family dynamic: my brother's suicide. My brother, who was a difficult person to be around in part because of his lack of social skills (Asperger's) and his upbringing, died by suicide last year, after suffering an acute delusional disorder during which he reached out for help from my dad's family. My dad neglected to do anything that would have helped him. This is what led to my final estrangement from my father.

What has helped? Time has helped. And severing the relationship. Trying to learn about myself and to change have also helped, as has having an incredibly supportive mother, sister, and husband. As to therapy or counseling, I haven't been in counseling much. When I was in my early 20s I was misdiagnosed as bipolar and put on lithium that I went off after a few months without accompanying counseling.

At the time that I was diagnosed as bipolar (a totally incorrect diagnosis) I was trying to deal with a sexual assault, as well. I've also had to deal with chronic depression and low self-esteem, both of which have so much to do with being steamrolled by an authoritarian figure: being told you don't matter, being rejected if you express your own opinion, and not being allowed to have your own emotional reactions to things or even your own likes and dislikes. To this day, whenever I go to buy ice cream, I think of how my dad never asked us what flavor we wanted and always bought his favorite, as if he was entitled.

As to making a break with my father, that came with both positives and negatives. It was positive in that I can see things more clearly, and I can understand how I spent most of my life seeing him as I wanted to see him, rather than as he truly was (that is, excusing his behavior and imagining a sort of benign version of him which pulled only on all his good traits). But there are negatives, too, in that I feel a lot of guilt, especially around holidays and birthdays, as if I'm the one who is to blame for not contacting him when he never tries to contact me. I also feel a lot of rejection, which I didn't feel before – this understanding that I must never have really mattered to him, if he can let go of me so easily.

That feeling of rejection makes me think of my brother, who my dad pretty much abandoned, only sending cards (and some money which, yes, was certainly appreciated) on holidays, and how my brother must have felt. He didn't tell my dad what my dad wanted to hear (Asperger's doesn't exactly support that kind of social savviness), which is partly what caused their rift, whereas I maintained our relationship for years by being the 'good girl,' making small talk, rarely expressing my opinion, and doing things like letting him choose the damn ice cream.

If I have any advice to give, I think it's the following: I think it's important to try to understand the reality of an authoritarian parent apart from how we viewed things as a child. I've realized – with distance from my father and with remembering the circumstances that I went through in my childhood – that I had essentially overlaid a fantasy version of my dad over the reality of the person he is. It took my brother's suicide (and my father's absolute lack of concern and atrocious, self-oriented behavior around his funeral) to puncture that layering so I could see things clearly.

This is essential for growth, I think, even though it brings with it grief over the parenting that I never had, feelings of abandonment, and a lot of feelings of low self-esteem, because I realize that I matter very little to him if he can't control me. There are some aspects of this wound that can never be healed. I think this pain and the constant striving to understand it have pushed me toward becoming a writer ... and they always influence the stories that I tell.

**

Authoritarians traumatize their victims. The idea of trauma-informed care is a relatively recent one, and we are just beginning to understand and honor the disabling long-term effects of trauma. The experience of Paula's sister in the following story may seem humorous – Paula says that she and her sister laugh about it – but you can bet that it was actually a traumatizing experience with long-lasting consequences. As a humane helper, you'll want to familiarize yourself with the concepts and tactics of trauma-informed care, concepts and tactics that we'll discuss in a future chapter. Here is Paula's story.

**

Authoritarians have been a constant in my life. First, there was my overbearing and critical father, followed by controlling people (bosses, coworkers, a spouse, and so-called friends) who somehow could sense that I had a lot of experience at being ... acquiescent. At the time, it was terrible to have my power diminished by somebody else. Now, still experiencing it as an older adult, I view it as something familiar that I watch in a deliberately cognizant way.

I'm not sure if my father was an authoritarian leader or an authoritarian follower. My father was actually a bit of a kiss-ass at work (an executive in a large corporation). But when he came home, he "left his fiddle at the door," as the Irish say. And my sister and I became very adept at reading his nonverbal movements, which showed us what kind of a day he'd had at work.

Weekends were agony for us as children, since my father ran the house like a military base, yelling out orders and berating us if we weren't quick enough. When he came home from work on weekdays during the summer, he'd ask in a rough, mean voice, "What did you DO all day?" as though we had to justify our existence – at the age of six! We became good at doing unnecessary chores, just for a list of things to provide him with at the end of the day.

Summer vacation was no vacation for US. It took a long time to learn how to relax during my free time as an adult ... I was a very tense child. I was the little white-haired girl with the worried anxious look in all the photos. My sister and I laugh about the story of a Saturday when we were children and my dad screamed at her to "get some elbow grease" when she was polishing his car for him. She ran to the garage, searching desperately through the bottles of brake fluid and Windex, crying her eyes out but unable to find the bottle marked "Elbow Grease."

I think I wilted under the constant pressure. What has helped? Well, time heals all wounds... a bit. Not accepting help from my father during college, when I worked lots of menial jobs so I wouldn't "owe" him anything, or when I finished college, where I took more menial jobs because I would not accept his help in getting me a job. Living in a different state and getting away physically. Of course, my parents moved to be closer to ME as they aged ... sigh. To this day, I am still berated for being a "failure."

When my father dies, it will be a huge relief – one less person to please! To break from other controllers, I have simply left the area or cut them off with no feelings of loss or guilt. Because they're not family, it is easy to do. I am the woman people always choose to sit next to on the bus (safe? boring?) and can make friends easily, but when I see the warning signs of someone – male or female – trying to control me, I cut off contact by being unavailable.

I was thinking the other day that I am angry that my father was NOT the kind of guy who would provide unconditional love and approval. That instead I was "given" a father who would constantly judge me, critique me, make me feel less than I was. I suppose growing up with that and continuing to this day to have to deal with that, I have become a mom who IS unconditionally loving and approving of her child. I appreciate people who do not look for gain in their contacts with others. I am wary of cons. I still wear an anvil on my head while my father is still demanding and – oh – pretty much impossible, but I keep my distance and tell my long-suffering mother, "Have fun with that!" since she has chosen to remain with him for all these years.

My advice? Value your true self. Be more discerning. Be more of a bitch! It is sad to have to become more self-protective, since you may be losing out on getting to know people who might enhance your life, but that self-protection is necessary. At this point, I can sense from the first few words of meeting someone as to whether they are truly kind and thoughtful or whether they are manipulative and only pretending to be nice. But it is sad that I have HAD to acquire this "super power."

* *

8

THE EXPLOITATION CLUSTER

One particular agenda defines the authoritarian personality: the hate-and-punish agenda I've described previously. Along with that agenda come three specific clusters of traits and qualities: an aggression cluster, an exploitation cluster, and a narcissism cluster. We've delved into the aggression cluster; in this chapter, we'll look at the traits and qualities that make up the exploitation cluster. In several subsequent chapters, we'll examine the exploitation cluster in more detail.

Authoritarians regularly exploit and make use of the people around them. Respondent Sara, for example, explained:

> My parents acknowledge my existence and my accomplishments exactly insofar as it benefits them. They treat me as if everything I do in my life is for them to exploit for their own social or personal advancement. If what I'm doing or who I'm in a relationship with doesn't benefit them or conform to their idea of success, they actively work to destroy it and attack me emotionally, no matter how happy I am and even though I am an adult.
>
> When I was in a relationship with a demonstratively abusive man, who was highly professionally accomplished, they encouraged and supported the relationship and closed their eyes to the obvious abuse. They still deny there was abuse and would like to see me together with him again, even though the relationship was horrible. Until I understood that they were exactly as exploitive as they are, their actions toward me and their positions vis-à-vis me made no sense. Now I understand completely.

Here are the 12 traits and qualities that make up the exploitation cluster.

Intrusiveness

When you combine an exploitive attitude, a need to control others, and a desire to shame and humiliate, you land on the following authoritarian trait: intrusiveness. Authoritarians are regularly "into your personal business," especially your sexual business and often your bathroom business, in improper and unacceptable ways.

Respondent Jill, for example, explained,

> For me, the abuse inflicted on me by my father was not physical but verbal and also something else that's hard to define. He was always saying "It's none of your business" and "You don't own anything in this house" and "Do as you're told!" And he was always banging on the bathroom door or barging in if I was in there too long. He'd come in yelling, his face all purple. It was a crazy way of life with us.

Manipulation

Authoritarians are typically Machiavellian. In classic fashion, they employ cunning and duplicity to reach their ends, ends that include domination, winning, looking good, and punishing their enemies. Machiavellianism is one of the "dark triads" of personality traits and has been researched by contemporary psychologists, who've developed measures to test for high Machiavellianism. What sorts of questions do "high Machs" agree with? "Never tell anyone the real reason you did something unless it is useful to do so." What sorts of questions do they disagree with? "Most people are basically good and kind" and "Most people who get ahead in the world lead clean, moral lives."

Research into their motivation indicates that they value money, power, and competition and devalue community and family. Respondent Ralph had this to add:

My brother had this cunning way about him from birth. Even as a two-year-old he could manipulate situations so that others got punished for no particular reason. He seemed to just simply enjoy seeing that happen. He wore a smile that you wanted to knock off his face. As he got older, he became more and more crooked in his dealings. One of his tricks stands out in my mind. He was a bad chess player, and he almost always found himself in the worse position. So, if you glanced away for a moment, he would make an illegal move, like having a bishop take a piece on the wrong color. When you called him on it he would go ballistic, which of course always ended with the board getting knocked over. A great way to never lose a chess game.

Shaming Efforts, Derision, and Ridicule

The hatred-and-punishment authoritarian agenda produces a person who takes pleasure in cruelty and who regularly shames, derides, and ridicules his current targets. To control is not enough; to win is not enough; to dominate is not enough: none of that is experienced as enough. The authoritarian wants you harmed and diminished. Since nothing feels quite as bad as shame, it is shame especially that the authoritarian wants you to experience.

As respondent Samantha put it,

> My father always looked at me as if I had no clothes on. I always felt naked around him. I don't know how he did it exactly; he didn't molest me or even touch me. In fact, he never touched me, not even to hug me. But what he did was almost worse and I always felt ashamed in his presence.

Rob explained,

> My father always shamed me in front of company. When we were just at home, I guess shaming me wasn't worth his time; he needed an audience. But when we went to the house of one of his friend's, then he would delight in ridiculing me.

Religiosity and Religious Cover

There are many reasons why authoritarians are typically either religious, claim to be religious, or get into bed with religion. You can expect either religious fervor and a heartfelt adoration of a spiteful, punishing God or else cynical religious posturing from the authoritarian in your client's life. We'll spend a whole chapter examining this dynamic, as it is so important and as it is under-examined in the authoritarian literature.

To take one example, here are respondent Larry's observations:

> I got so sick and tired of my stepfather throwing what he called his "Bible rules" at me that I figured out a small test that anyone who's read the Bible would be able to answer. I said to him, "Do you even know the Bible?" When he claimed that he did, I said, "Prove it." I asked him the first question. He clearly had no idea what the answer was; he exploded and gave me the beating of my life. I almost enjoyed it, because I knew that he knew that he'd been exposed as a liar and a hypocrite. After that, he still attacked us with his Bible rules, but he was somehow much less convincing.

Anti-Intellectualism and Anti-Rationalism

The sorts of explanations that clear thinking, the scientific method, and the application of reason provide do not suit the authoritarian agenda. Science will not help you think that you are special when you are not; clear thinking will not help you scapegoat others; the application of reason puts the lie to your lies. Therefore, it follows that authoritarians abhor education, especially science and critical thinking, and punish their victims for daring to think.

Authoritarians who acquire political power immediately take direct aim at the academics, scientists, writers, and other thinkers in their society, often terrorizing, killing, or forcing to flee even those professionals their society really needs, like its doctors. Authoritarians are immediately and virulently antagonistic to any rational argument and to anyone who thinks rationally, making communication with an authoritarian bewildering for someone who supposes that reasonable arguments ought to persuade and ought to matter. This dynamic is important enough that we'll spend an upcoming chapter on it.

Hypocrisy

Hypocrisy is a hallmark quality of authoritarians, who love rules for others but who typically despise them for themselves. As respondent Ayanna explained,

> My father was Islamic and a hypocrite. He expected us children and his wife to follow all the rules but broke many of them himself. He would pretend to follow some. Both he and my mother used physical violence against us kids. My father beat us regularly with a belt. He also got madder during a beating if we tried to protect ourselves with our hands or if we cried. My mother would always watch the beatings, gleefully. But what stands out for me is the hypocrisy.

Respondent Alfred explained,

> My grandmother always preached that we should live by 'high standards.' For her, this meant keeping the part of her house that you could see immaculately clean – she waxed and polished those floors every day – and keeping her private spaces as dirty as pigsties. If by chance you wandered into one of those spaces she'd scream at you and hit you with her broom and then make believe that none of it ever happened. And she would go right back to preaching her 'high standards.'

Diminishment

Authoritarians have a powerful need to discount your dreams, belittle your accomplishments, and make you feel small, inferior, and less than. These are all faces of their hate-and-punish agenda. As respondent Deborah described it,

> My father was authoritarian through and through with our mother, my twin sister, and me. When I told him that I wanted to get a PhD in philosophy, his response was "And

then what will you do, think while you carry the mail?" Somehow these comments made my career decisions for me. Years later he sent me some of his old papers. One of them was a letter written to the Peace Corps saying, "Deborah is not a leader." Why did he say that when in my high school yearbook, I had 26 leadership activities under my name? And why did he need me to see what he'd written to the Peace Corps?

Prejudice and Bigotry

If your motivation is hate and your agenda is to punish, you require objects for both. Why not hate whole groups and wish for them all to be punished? One fascinating result from the research on the authoritarian personality is the eager willingness of authoritarians to hate and punish even *their own group*. On the face of it, this sounds absurd. But since an authoritarian lacks empathy, compassion, fellow-feeling, loyalty, and any other quality that might make him care about some group, his own group included, this isn't actually surprising.

This hatred of and desire to punish whole groups – women, Jews, gypsies, homosexuals, the infirm, the elderly, etc. – plays itself out as prejudice and bigotry, two natural and inevitable consequences of the authoritarian agenda. This is the most public face of fascism and of authoritarian leadership – that whole groups are a menace, inferior, or both, and need punishing – and a regular subject of conversation for everyday authoritarians. These prejudices and bigotries may have played themselves out dramatically in your client's life: for example, by your client marrying someone of another race as an act of rebellion and a repudiation of his or her parents' values.

Preoccupation with Sex and Promiscuity

Authoritarians, who are filled with hate, hate it that anyone (themselves sometimes excepted and themselves sometimes included) is enjoying sex or being sexual. Respondent Roberta remembered:

The authoritarian personality in my mother did not emerge until I hit puberty. I had no idea what was coming. The second I began expressing an interest in boys she became hypervigilant, watching my every word and my every move. She also became violently aggressive in ways that she had never been before, for example, smacking me with the rolled-up magazines I began reading. It was like a monster had appeared on the scene.

Cynicism

Authoritarians hold to the view that it's a dog-eat-dog world and cynically presume that everyone is essentially as ruthless, exploitative, and self-serving as they are. As respondent Jack put it,

> My boss had several pet expressions, all of them sexual and sadistic. One was, "Do it to them first – and harder!" Another was, "Come from behind – never let them see you coming!" His favorite was, "If they're not screaming, you're not winning!" He made more money than anybody, bought a penthouse apartment, and came on to his friends' girlfriends and wives – nothing gave him more pleasure than that. He loved it and it completely matched his cynical picture of life that so many of them ended up betraying their man with him. That really cemented his worldview!

Love of Chaos and Disasters

Authoritarians love it when those around them are caught off balance and kept off balance, as those distracted and vulnerable others are then that much easier to exploit. They love natural disasters, personal disasters, the chaos of political upheaval, the chaos of serious illness, the chaos of economic catastrophes, and anything else that weakens, confuses, or disorients their potential victims.

Respondent Adam explained,

> The first thing my father said when I lost my job was that he saw it coming, that I never should have chosen the career I chose,

that I didn't understand how to be a man in a man's world, and that of course he wouldn't help me financially, as I still hadn't learned how to stand on my own two feet. What stood out for me was how much joy he got out of saying all of that. It was as if it was the best thing that had happened to him in the longest time. I haven't spoken to him since – and he hasn't reached out to me, even though my kids are his only grandchildren.

Deception

Authoritarians regularly exploit through deception. Respondent Matt explained,

> My wife liked to use the following bait-and-switch tactic. She would offer to take time off from her high-powered corporate work for a family vacation if I would do all the planning for the trip. I would then do that, in part because the planning was fun and exciting – and then she would announce that she couldn't take the time off. She knew that giving me the chance to plan would occupy me and keep me from complaining about how little time we spent together. This was completely deceptive on her part because she never blocked off that time – it was a complete lie from beginning to end – I learned that inadvertently from her secretary.

Many of the above 12 traits and qualities are instantly recognizable and easy to understand. A few are less obvious and deserve more attention. In the next chapter, we look at how authoritarians exploit ignorance, and in the chapter after that we examine how authoritarians exploit religion. These chapters will help you better understand why your victimized clients may have had lifelong problems in the areas of education and career, lifelong challenges seeing themselves as smart or capable, and lifelong confusion about how to meet their spiritual and existential needs, given how religion may have been weaponized in their family of origin.

9

EXPLOITING IGNORANCE

Authoritarians want people to remain ignorant and then they exploit that ignorance.

The authoritarians in question may be educators, they may have advanced degrees, or they may have a high intelligence, but their hate-and-punish agenda is vastly helped if the people around them remain in the Dark Ages. If, for example, you have a vested interest in portraying a certain group as inferior, so that you can punish them, would you want anyone to know about that group's accomplishments? If you wanted a free hand to pollute, would you want anyone to know about the toxicity of their drinking water? The less people know, the better authoritarians fare. Authoritarians know this, which is why they are uniformly anti-education, anti-rationality, and anti-intellectual.

A victim of authoritarian wounding may never quite realize a headline truth about his life and environment: "Little thinking allowed here." Likewise, he may be surprised to learn just how deep this antipathy runs. In most societies, thought is not just disparaged; the thinking person is targeted as an enemy of the people. He is mocked as elitist and effete, his progressive views are hated, and if he lives in a society run by tyrants, he will be silenced and may be imprisoned or murdered. This has happened throughout history, continues to this day, and is a fundamental aspect of authoritarianism. Ignorance always has been and always will be something that authoritarians exploit.

Tyrants hate intellectuals, since intellectuals as a class see tyranny for what it is and can articulate what they see. Intellectuals know when freedom is being violated and stolen. They are better attuned to knowing that they are being fed lies. They recognize to what extent the majority opinion is an anti-intellectual one. To take one small example occurring as I write this, Republican legislators in Texas are trying to have the teaching of critical thinking skills banned from public schools in Texas. Anti-intellectualism is society-wide and may have had a much greater effect on your wounded client than he or she knows.

Attacks on thinking and attacks on smart people occur all the time. Here is one report from contemporary Iraq, as reported by the watchdog group "A Face and a Name: Civil Victims of Insurgent Groups in Iraq":

> Some Iraqi academics see the current attacks as a way to destroy Iraq's intellectual elite. Precise figures are difficult to obtain, but studies suggest that doctors and academics are particularly at risk. A study by the Iraqi Ministry of Health concluded that armed groups have abducted between 160 and 300 Iraqi doctors since April 2003 and killed more than twenty-five. Nearly 1,000 doctors have fled the country, the study said, with an average of thirty more following each month. To stem the outflow, the ministry broadcast a public service announcement on television in spring 2005, with a message that said: "Dear Citizens, please do not kill doctors – you may need them one day."
>
> Professors at Iraq's once prestigious universities are also under attack. According to an April 2005 United Nations University report, assassins have killed forty-eight academics since 2003, and many more teachers and professors brave daily threats. Hundreds of academics and professionals have been threatened with death and told to leave Iraq. According to the Association of University Teachers, 2,000 professors have left Iraq since 2003, joining the 10,000 professors the association says left the country in the twelve years after the Gulf War.

Attacks on people who can think occur in every culture and in every epoch. Rebellious feminists in Russia are labeled with mental disorders made up on the spot for the purposes of incarcerating them. Scientists who point out the environmental dangers caused by business are ridiculed as fearmongers. Every age and every culture has its versions of cultural revolutions, inquisitions, and Scopes trials. How can a child who is born smart and born into an authoritarian household have any inkling that her abilities are likely to be disparaged, that thinking itself will be envied and hated by many in her society, or that she may be targeted by her government – or her parents – because she wants to think or, worse yet, wants to enter a thinking profession?

A child brought up in an anti-intellectual, anti-rational, and anti-education environment likely will not think much, even though she has the ability to think, and when confronted by tasks that require her to think, she will find herself too anxious and too unprepared to meet the rigors of thinking. As a result, she will fail, disappoint herself, dream small, and begin to form an identity that includes a huge doubt about whether she is as smart as she thought she was. This child is bound to grow sad, act out, or sabotage herself and show the "symptoms" of one "mental disorder" or another, from "childhood depression" to "attention deficit disorder" to "obsessive-compulsive disorder."

These negative outcomes are predictable. They are exactly what you would expect to see if at every turn you prevented a child from thinking freely and deeply. If you put a good brain in a brain-unfriendly environment, it should not surprise you to see that brain get sad (a state that will eventually get labeled "chronic depression"), respond impulsively and carelessly rather than thoughtfully, say by marrying young, getting pregnant young, or dropping out of school, doubt its abilities and its options, and choose a station in life a notch or two below the one it might otherwise have chosen.

Respondent Mark explained:

> I was pushed by my father to work with my hands, stay away from books, and especially to stay away from science. It was such a strange thing, because I needed to know basic

mechanics to fix cars, and he was all for that, but if I wanted to know anything more scientific than that I got screamed at. He was always making the distinction between "things you need to know" and "things you don't need to know." I needed to know scripture (he claimed to know it, but he really didn't) but I didn't need to know history. I needed to know how things worked, but if I went one inch over the line and showed any curiosity in book learning, the belt appeared. I once asked him, "Can I be an engineer?" and he flew off the handle. "You'll work in a garage," he screamed, "you'll go to church, and you'll have a family!" I ended up pretty much unemployable.

Respondent Alice shared the following story:

My mother had her PhD in art history. She was a failed painter who had done the whole Paris and New York thing, gotten her degrees, and then came back to our small town to lick her wounds and have a family. She came around to hating art, hating the idea of education, and hating any train of thought that took more than a few seconds to finish. If one of us – there were three children – tried to explain anything, she would yell, "Stop explaining!" "Explaining" was like the dirtiest word to her. I once came home excited about the dinosaur extinction – I was probably in third grade and we had just seen a film on the meteorite that hit Mexico and killed all the dinosaurs – and tried to tell my mother about it. She went ballistic! "Good riddance to them!" she shouted. It was one of the weirdest things I have ever heard anyone say about anything. It of course followed that when I graduated from college she refused to attend the ceremony, announcing that I had "wasted my time and gone into debt" for no good reason.

Respondent Margaret explained:

In my town we had an extreme divide between town and gown. The university just outside of town was like the devil incarnate to my parents. They hated the teachers, hated the students, and charged them with everything from public uncleanliness to sexual perversions to wholesale moral bankruptcy. Our city council floated a law that no more than three students could come into town together – the most insane law of all time, modeled, I think, on those signs outside of candy stores that only three kids could come in at a time – and my parents were all over it, working day and night for its passage. It did pass – and just about the whole university came into town together in protest. My father had to be restrained from getting out his shotgun. I never could understand that unbelievable animosity, except that now I can begin to connect it to his authoritarian nature and the way he loved ignorance.

You can help your clients understand that the harm they experienced likely included this particular harm. With your help, your client can learn how to tolerate the anxiety that now accompanies her efforts at thinking. She can seize "thinking" as a meaning opportunity and make conscious meaning investments in some "thinking domain," whether it's a profession that she thought was out of her reach or a body of knowledge that she would love to study, but didn't dare begin for fear of failing. She can be helped to understand that she never was "stupid" but rather was made as stupid as possible by the authoritarians in her life. With your help, these are the sort of insights she can gain and the sorts of changes that she can commence to make.

You can also help her prepare for recontact and deal with ongoing contact. If she goes back to spend a day with her family, she will again have to deal with that anti-thinking environment. If she has not left her church, she will have to deal with that ongoing anti-thinking environment. If her friends sneer at thinking, she will have to deal with them. If she turns on the television to relax, she will have to deal with the anti-thinking programming filling every channel. That she heroically works on herself won't prevent environmental factors from continuing their mischief and mayhem, and you can help her prepare for that inevitable recontact and ongoing contact.

Clients who look for psychological help are often the smartest folks around. A smart person has a desire to think, a need to think, and an ability to think. But the nature of family, school, and work, the structure of society, and the proclivities of the people around him, authoritarians especially, often conspire to put out his intellectual fire. His family is unlikely to inspire him or flame his desire to think; school is unlikely to inspire him; his job is unlikely to inspire him; his pastor is unlikely to inspire him; mass entertainment and his other relaxations are unlikely to inspire him; and the uninteresting conversations around him are unlikely to inspire him. You can help point this out and aid your clients in fanning their own intellectual flames.

You can also help point out the following, which your clients were probably aware of just outside of conscious awareness but may have never considered consciously. You can point out that the education system itself has held them back and harmed them. At first glance, it might seem absurd that society should intentionally choose to poorly educate its children. Yet there is a strong pull in our culture to do just that. The reason is a straightforward one. Most people – and authoritarians especially, including those who get onto school boards – do not want children to think. They want children to obey, fit in, find a job, play sports, salute the flag, kneel in prayer – but not think. Those who want to preserve their privileges, whether it's their drinking habits, their bank accounts, or their fairy tales, do not want their children or any children to ask difficult questions, dispute authority, or threaten them with exposure by knowing too much or learning too much.

The self-interest of most adults – especially authoritarians – makes them secretly wish that all schools would crumble and vanish. This is why so little critical thinking is taught in schools. Educators agree at the level of lip service that teaching critical thinking skills is education's number one priority. Yet classroom observers report that in over 95% of the classrooms they visit, no critical thinking skills are taught. This is understandable, as an unspoken agreement has been reached by everyone involved – by parents, politicians, school board members, school superintendents, principals, and, reluctantly and against their better judgment, teachers – that thinking is dangerous and should not be countenanced.

Often "learning" is countenanced, even by some authoritarians. Learning is relatively safe, certainly safer than thinking. Fewer feathers are ruffled if you provide your students with another plane geometry theorem or 20 new French vocabulary words. The system is set up to support exactly this sort of transaction. There is a school subject called plane geometry, there is plane geometry subject matter, there is a teacher who teaches plane geometry, there is a student who learns plane geometry and is tested in plane geometry, there are uses for plane geometry, as a pillar in a liberal education and a stepping stone to solid geometry, and it all makes perfect, seamless sense. Doesn't it? Yes: if one of your goals is to minimize thinking and substitute learning instead.

A child who grows up in an anti-intellectual home and a culture that disparages thinking, actively works to shut it down at every turn, and begins to track him and tell him what he's good for and what is beyond his reach, will then find himself in the jaws of his society's work machinery. He will be fit for one sort of job and not another, he will be aimed into one social class and not another, and he will find himself with limited, disappointing options with lifelong consequences. Here is how Jonathan in England explained it:

> Where I live there is a 'life tracking' effect in place, where if you happen to be somehow put on the wrong 'track' as regards your intelligence, it can be a nightmare trying to put it straight later in life. If you leave school because you feel like you are on the wrong track and not being served by school, how can you ever redevelop the self-esteem that has been robbed from you or ever make it through a degree program as if everything had all been fine and dandy.

It can take years to recover from such a mauling, and even when the emotional and personal side of things is resolved, there is still the matter of no degree and no proper career.

Unfortunately, industry and academia both act as if the highest level of educational attainment that was available to a person when young represents the maximum worth of their mind. That's kind of tough when it wasn't your fault. The unresolved situation in my case is a lack of a suitable career that taps into my interests and aptitudes. I am getting older and remain a highly gifted autodidact unsuccessfully searching for a job in the neurosciences.

The headline to take away from this chapter is that clients who have been wounded by authoritarian contact are likely to have lifelong problems connected to the ways in which their home life and their culture were (or still are) anti-education, anti-rationality, and anti-intellectual. This harm will play itself out in all sorts of ways: one client may have failed to find interesting, intellectually nourishing work, another may have always thought of himself as "stupid," a third may grow highly anxious whenever asked to think (including if asked to think in session). You will want to remain alert to these possibilities and realities.

10

EXPLOITING RELIGION AND RELIGIOSITY

Authoritarians exploit people. They exploit people they know, like family members; people they do not know, like customers harmed by their business practices; classes of people, like children or the poor; those they claim to love, like their own children; and those they salivate at hating. However, in addition to exploiting individuals and groups, they also regularly exploit circumstances, institutions, and anything else that might serve their purposes.

A fascist coming to power perfectly suits their hate-and-punish agenda and is an event they will rush to exploit. A war can be exploited through war profiteering, a disease can be exploited by raising drug prices, an attack can be exploited as a way to vilify a whole culture. A business rival's misstep will be quickly exploited: an authoritarian would find it pathetic and ridiculous to do otherwise. The same with a tax loophole: to not take it would seem ludicrous. Authoritarians are always on the lookout for circumstances that they can exploit.

Likewise, authoritarians exploit institutions. Religion and the military are two institutions that they naturally love. They love the idea of someone giving orders and others obliged to take orders; they love the idea of strict punishments, like courts-martial and hellfire; they love the hierarchal nature of such institutions and forced gestures, like saluting and kneeling; and they love the permission such institutions give you to hate others, all those millions of enemies and infidels.

Of course, authoritarians may also avoid the military like the plague and not believe in gods in the least – remember that cynicism and hypocrisy are also hallmark qualities of authoritarians. But they love the authoritarian flavor of such institutions and intuitively understand that they ought to align with them, at least publicly. That's why authoritarian nonbelievers who seek public office will profess a belief in gods in which they don't believe and a love of religion which they never demonstrate.

The research has consistently linked religiosity with authoritarianism. Few findings are as robust or as consistently replicated. For instance, the psychologists Hunsberger and Laurier, in their research article "Religion and Prejudice: The Role of Religious Fundamentalism, Quest, and Right-Wing Authoritarianism" (*in the Journal of Social Issues*), explained:

> Does religion contribute to, or inhibit, prejudice? Although major world religions espouse tolerance and love toward others, empirical evidence provides little support for the effectiveness of such religious teachings, and a considerable body of research suggests that religion and prejudice are positively correlated. Further, the fundamentalism and quest relationships with prejudice are especially meaningful in light of an association with right-wing authoritarianism.

Bob Altemeyer, one of the most important researchers in the area of the authoritarian personality, explained in "Authoritarianism, Religious Fundamentalism, Quest, and Prejudice" (in the *International Journal for the Psychology of Religion*):

> Five studies of university students and their parents were carried out to investigate the relationships among right-wing authoritarianism, various indices of religious orientation, and prejudice. Measures of religious fundamentalism, developed for this research, proved to be psychometrically sound, and were good discriminators between prejudiced and unprejudiced persons, across a variety of different measures

of prejudice and authoritarian aggression. Apparently, religious fundamentalism is linked with authoritarianism and prejudice toward a wide variety of minority groups.

Since authoritarians are full of hate and a need to punish, it is crystal clear why they would be drawn to the world's religions, whose motifs are hatred and not love, control and not freedom, and punishment and not compassion. Naturally the fundamentalist end of each religion will contain the most virulent authoritarians; and the research is again clear that this is the case.

For example, Philip Perry in "Is There a Link Between Religiosity and Authoritarianism?" (for Bigthink.com), in reviewing the research literature on the connection between authoritarianism and religiosity, made the following observations:

> Religions preach peace, tolerance, love, and understanding. But a growing body of evidence shows that those who tend to be very religious, often bend towards authoritarianism. Fundamentalists seem to have the strongest association with authoritative ideas. This includes traits such as respect for social order, submission to authority and conventionality, and an intolerance for outside groups. In fact, this link has been studied by political scientists, psychologists, and social scientists since the 1950s. According to a 1995 study, in the Journal for the Scientific Study of Religion, those who identify as religious tend to be authoritarian, and authoritarians tend to be religious.
>
> Research published in 2007 in that same journal found a strong correlation with consistent attendance at religious services and strong feelings of religious affiliation with intolerance, prejudice, authoritarianism, and dogmatism. Fundamentalists with unwavering commitment to religious teachings were found to be the most authoritarian. A 2011 meta-analysis found that fundamentalism correlated positively with authoritarianism, ethnocentrism, militarism, and prejudice.

For both authoritarian leaders and authoritarian followers, religion is a wonderful convenience. It allows them to lord it over other people, since they alone know the truth. It allows them to punish people guilt-free, since that punishment is on a god's orders. It allows them to deny reason by dubbing the irrational "faith." It gives them extra ways to bully people, especially women, who are regularly regarded as second class. It is just about everything an authoritarian could wish for.

Many authoritarians, both on the right and on the left, do not believe in the gods they profess to believe in but still love the cover of religion. They know that to associate with a religion is to associate with like-minded authoritarians. To take a classic example, the atheistic, anticlerical Mussolini, so as to get into bed with the Vatican, married in church, had his children baptized, and in his first parliamentary speech in 1921 announced that "the only universal values that radiate from Rome are those of the Vatican." Mussolini knew where he would find his fascistic friends and allies: in church.

To take another example from the same time period, when the fascist-leaning, anticlerical Futurist artist Marinetti, who had once said of the Catholic Church that "throughout its history the Vatican has defecated on Italy," saw the value of aligning himself and the Futurist movement with "the sacred," he decided to create a "Manifesto of Futurist Sacred Art" and to participate in the Vatican's International Exhibition of Sacred Art. Writers, painters, doctors, lawyers, butchers, bakers are not above such shenanigans – no authoritarian is above such shenanigans.

Religions are by their nature authoritarian. They castigate the other and designate the other as deserving of punishment, they demand strict obedience, they reduce nuanced discourse to the size of slogans, and they announce that they are the chosen ones, the anointed ones, and owners of the future. Therefore, they align beautifully with individual authoritarian agendas. An individual authoritarian spouting the sanctimonious homilies of a religion is a marriage made in Heaven.

Indeed, fascism, that authoritarian extreme, has been dubbed a "political religion" because of the way its mimics orthodox religion. Popularized by Emilio Gentile, the term "political religion" refers to any movement that sacralizes itself and adopts the trappings of religion, including religion's emphasis on the neverending battle between good and evil. These trappings can be found in every sort of group and institution, from corporations to fraternal clubs to professional organizations … and of course in families. As to the ways in which religious trappings are employed by family authoritarians, here are three characteristic responses from respondents to my Authoritarian Wound Questionnaire.

Respondent Rachel explained,

> I grew up in an orthodox Jewish home. I learned that I was dirty, unworthy, expendable, and second-class. I learned that nothing could be questioned and that no rational reason was needed to justify the edicts of my father and mother. The worst was when the religious men gathered. They felt to me like a pack of wild animals. You just knew that they would tear you apart given half the chance.
>
> Once, when we had a group over to our house, I tried to say something nice about the honey sponge cake that my mother served – I only wanted to say that it was very good. But because I interrupted a visiting rabbi who was speaking I got slammed across the face. I've had dental problems my whole life from that incident.

Respondent Aabida explained,

> My father was a Muslim and my mother was Catholic. They were both authoritarians and religious zealots. Because of their religious beliefs, they started looking for a husband for me when I was eleven years old. My mother, who was raised by nuns in an orphanage, parented us the way she was raised. We were not permitted to ask any questions,

and we were beaten for talking too loudly or talking at all at the table when my father was praying.

Once my father got up from his prayers, beat the table with his belt, and broke what everyone thought was an unbreakable plate. A flying piece of the plate split my three-year-old sister's eyebrow open. We had many religious responsibilities, many family meetings, and when my sisters and I got older my father tried to get our brothers to also beat us, but they refused. So, they were beaten instead. That was our life.

Respondent Anne explained,

When my older sister was twenty-two, she announced that she was going to get married. My parents hated the boy, but the worst part was … he was an atheist! My mother, who had always announced that only a church wedding would do, insisted that no clergy would marry them if he was atheist. Well, they found one. But that didn't matter. My parents refused to give their blessing to a marriage to an atheist. And my sister refused to back down.

On the night that they kicked my sister out, I was awakened by the commotion. I went downstairs to find my sister loading her possessions into her car. I asked what was going on. My mother responded, "Your sister refuses to live by our rules so she has to leave. And you have to decide, are you loyal to her or to me? If you're loyal to her, then you're going right out there with her!" There I was, ten years old, having to make a decision like that!

Religious followers are more antidemocratic then their secular brothers and sisters and followers of orthodox sects are even more antidemocratic. In the classic 1950s book on the subject of authoritarians, *The Authoritarian Personality*, Theodor Adorno and his University of California at Berkeley colleagues explained:

There is reason to believe that individuals, out of their needs to conform and to belong and to believe and through such devices as imitation and conditioning, often take over more or less ready-made the opinions, attitudes, and values that are characteristic of the groups in which they have membership. To the extent that the ideas which prevail in such a group are implicitly or explicitly antidemocratic, the individual group member might be expected to be receptive to propaganda having the same general direction.

This love affair between authoritarians and religion plays itself out in the lives of the victims of authoritarian contact in the following sorts of ways. A child is threatened with eternal damnation for not completing her chores. An adult child is banished from the house for coming out as gay. A child's accusations against his priest are ridiculed. An adult child is disowned for no longer believing. In each of these instances, the authoritarian's true nature is revealed. He is provided with permission to punish, permission to ridicule, permission to disown, and all the other permissions he craves by the religion with which he has chosen to align.

Authoritarians will naturally gravitate toward the more punitive sects within their religion and the more authoritarian practices of their religion. The authoritarian Buddhist will revere strict sitting and will love the idea of smacking squirming meditators with a stick. The authoritarian Catholic will argue for the Pope's infallibility. The authoritarian Jew will argue for a scriptural right to seize land. The authoritarian Hindu will pine for the heyday of the caste system and the banished practice of untouchability. Whatever door a religion allows for cruelty, authoritarians will flock through that door.

Your client who was in close contact with an authoritarian likely found the authoritarian's religious beliefs and religious posturing perplexing, bewildering, and frightening. He or she may have likewise sensed, quite rightly, that the authoritarian possessed no real belief in his god, didn't fear his god's wrath, and cared nothing for ideas like love, mercy, and compassion. Your client may have likewise sensed, again quite rightly, that for the authoritarian religion was just an added justification and additional excuse to be mean.

Whether the authoritarian in your client's life was using religion to further his ends, like a Mussolini, whether he was born into a religion, taught antidemocratic and authoritarian principles there, and indoctrinated into an authoritarian personality, whether he actually believed in gods or just had an affinity for the authoritarian nature of religion, however it is that he came to make that marriage, the result for your client will have been the same: harshness and cruelty justified by doctrine and dressed up in piety.

This is not an easy matter to discuss in session, as we are trained not to talk about religious beliefs. Indeed, your client may have adopted the authoritarian's religion, may possess fundamentalist religious beliefs of his or her own, and may resent any such line of inquiry. Nevertheless, you can inquire carefully by asking questions, like the following two: "Did your father's religious beliefs seem to connect to his authoritarian nature?" or "Do you think your mother was more or less of an authoritarian because of her religious beliefs?"

Even if this line of inquiry initially upsets your client, it may prove ultimately helpful. Respondents regularly reported that they had no idea where the authoritarian in their life was "coming from" when it came to religion and that it was both enlightening and healing to realize that religion was just another weapon in their authoritarian's hate-and-punish arsenal. If your client receives this as religion bashing and wants no part of it, you know how to stop. But if he or she is eager to better understand what went on, then you will have opened an important door that might otherwise have remained locked forever.

11

SOME CAT TOYS AND FREEDOM

Authoritarian exploitation takes on all sorts of forms. Respondents report how an aging authoritarian mother exploits her own weakness, how an authoritarian sister exploits her position as the least loved child, how an authoritarian child exploits the guilty feelings his antisocial behaviors provoke in his parents. In the following respondent's story, the authoritarian in question exploits his cancer as a way to manipulate and control his girlfriend. Should we expect an authoritarian who is dying to exhibit more compassion or conscience than a robust authoritarian in the prime of life? Respondents say no.

Authoritarians often act in more authoritarian ways as their circumstances worsen. Feeling unfairly treated by life, their hatred increases, as does their need to punish. Their victims are likely to become more enmeshed (say, with the needs of an aging authoritarian parent), feel more guilt (say, at the antics of an authoritarian child), and find separating from the authoritarian in question all that more difficult. These are dynamics that you, as a helper, can point out.

As helpers, we may find ourselves confused and perplexed as to why our client is still staying with an authoritarian boyfriend or girlfriend. We may find it a little easier to understand staying with a husband or wife, especially when there are children in the picture. But why stay with the boyfriend or girlfriend who is controlling you, abusing you, exploiting you, and making your life miserable? Typically, your client will prove at a loss to explain his or her misplaced loyalty. Even if you can't get at the why of it, however, you can still help your client move toward freedom, the sort of freedom Adele describes in the following story.

* *

My ex-boyfriend was highly volatile and controlling. It may be interesting or useful to note that he was 15 years older than me and actively receiving treatment for incurable cancer (multiple myeloma). He had a strained relationship with his family and by the time we broke up, he had alienated, insulted, and/or lost most of his friends and acquaintances.

It became increasingly difficult to be around him. We were together for about three and a half years, which I now look back on as far too long given how he treated me. He had a serious anger issue that he never fully addressed. He thought he was very emotionally and psychologically well adjusted, though he wasn't, and he exhibited many narcissistic traits – he was very full of himself and thought he was always right.

He controlled my personal and social life, insisting that I limit contact with friends he didn't like, and at one point he literally screamed at my best friend on the streets of New York City for some imagined slight. He didn't want me to be friends with my college boyfriend on Facebook and was generally unsupportive of me having an outside social life. As the relationship progressed, he became increasingly critical and aggressive. He would constantly criticize my actions, even simple ones like forgetting to refill a prescription or not entering a detailed enough description in a Google calendar event.

He made me start to believe that there was something wrong with me, that I was incompetent or incapable to a certain degree. I started therapy at his behest to try to "cure" my flaws. I am still on antidepressants for anxiety and depression. He would also lash out and on many occasions berated me – SCREAMED at me – throwing insults and making threats that if I did not improve my behavior (which was essentially my caretaking of him) he would break up with me.

He regularly made this threat in the last year or so of the relationship, but boy was he surprised when I finally left. A good friend helped me see that I was not crazy; he was abusive and I did not deserve that treatment. He would become violent sometimes, though not at me. He would scream, throw things. He once threw his phone as hard as he could at the wall across the room and it shattered. Of course, he blamed me for the broken phone.

I felt trapped toward the end. When he was angry, he wouldn't allow me to leave. I learned to become numb to his yelling. The dog would cower, absolutely petrified, whenever he got like this, but he blamed me for the dog being scared because I was the reason he was angry. This really upset me, but I couldn't really argue because he was never wrong. No matter what I said, he had an answer to explain why I was wrong, and he always controlled the situation so that he could get what he wanted and I had to stay and listen to him until he got it. If I tried to leave, step away, or cool down, he would threaten to break up with me.

Jack was an authoritarian leader, in my opinion, rather than an authoritarian follower. In his professional career, he worked his way up to an executive position. He grew up rather poor, so it was very important for him to have and maintain his high status. He struggled when he had to quit his job to focus on cancer treatment and desperately tried to hold on to symbols of status (high-rise apartment, fancy car, extravagant dinners) as they became increasingly irrational to maintain. He later tried starting his own business and was good at recruiting partners until he alienated them all by insulting them, not recognizing their accomplishments, and getting angry at their mistakes – exactly how he treated me.

As a result of all this I became a meek, self-conscious, frightened little girl. I had never been depressed before meeting Jack, but I still take antidepressants to this day. It has been over two years since I left, which was incredibly hard to do because of his gaslighting. He made me believe, and I still struggle with this today, that there was something inherently wrong with me. He actually made me believe that (in his words) I had a learning disability. I had zero confidence and no social life. I minimized contact with my parents, family, and old friends because I couldn't tell them how bad the relationship was – and I thought that it was my fault it was bad.

I abandoned my hobbies, personal interests, and certain values in order to spend every moment with him and not upset him by doing something he didn't agree with. I damaged friendships with two of my closest companions because of my relationship with Jack. I am in a wonderful, healthy relationship now, but I feel like some of these old wounds have affected my perception. Though my current partner never makes threats about leaving, I sometimes worry that I am not good enough – that he too will inevitably break up with me because my personal flaws and incompetence are so glaring. I also experience regular moments of self-doubt, low self-esteem, and shame. (Shaming me was a tactic Jack often employed.)

Leaving the relationship is still the best decision I've ever made. Being away from Jack and on my own completely changed my perspective and allowed me to see, finally, from the outside, just how wrong the relationship was. Talking with friends helped as well. Having freedom and full control over my own actions felt amazing. I no longer had to worry about Jack's moods. It felt refreshing once I started dating again, not only to have access to more social contact but to see that Jack's behavior was not normal and I was in fact a perfectly normal, capable, and desirable woman.

More than anything, having my own space – both physically and mentally – allowed me to remember that I was my own person in control of my own actions, and this helped me heal more than anything. I can't describe the liberating feeling of unloading all of the baggage that came with Jack and the relationship. I felt capable of taking on the world. And even though he was persistent and begged to get back together at first, at times wildly inappropriately (grabbing my purse and pulling me back into his car when I was trying to exit), he could not bring me down anymore. For the first time in years I felt close to happy, and more importantly, in control of my own destiny.

I did engage in therapy. I've talked about this situation with a therapist and with my psychiatrist. I wish I had been able to attend therapy more regularly both during and right after the relationship ended. I actually sometimes avoided going because of my issues with Jack – I think he realized that talking to someone might make me see things differently, which would hurt his control over me. It was helpful to discuss it in therapy for the same reason it was helpful to talk to friends about it; to be told and to understand that I was not crazy. Having this reassurance helped me process the negative feelings from the relationship and gave me confidence to move forward.

I received a depression diagnosis and an anxiety diagnosis, problems caused, I believe, by being with Jack. I never received nor needed treatment before meeting Jack. In fact, he was the one who requested I see a therapist because he was quite sure I had a learning disability (I have never been diagnosed as such and am unlikely to be). I am still taking medication, and I still struggle with my self-worth.

To repeat, leaving was the best choice I made. I did have feelings of guilt, but I think the positive far outweighed the negative of guilt feelings. My friend had to help me "escape," because I knew I couldn't talk to Jack about it – I knew he would never let me leave. I had already found a new apartment, signed the lease, and put down the deposit. One night, when Jack went to have a drink with a buddy, I called my friend, packed a bag, put my cat in his carrier, and she picked me up and drove me to my new apartment. I sent Jack a message telling him that I was done and had left.

I felt guilty about sneaking around this way and deceiving him, but I knew it was the only way, and it worked! So, it was hard to feel too bad about it. To this day, I am so grateful for my friend's help. I don't know if I could have done it without her. She was the first person to see the relationship dynamics firsthand (she was actually hired by Jack to be a personal assistant) and the only person to tell me that his treatment of me was not okay and that I did not have to stand for it. The only negative feelings I experienced during the breakup came from my interactions with Jack to settle our affairs, in which he treated me just as badly and reminded me why I had left. But the feelings of peaceful bliss helped me to not get sucked back into his trap.

I slept the first night away from him in a nearly empty apartment – just a borrowed air mattress, a couple of cat toys, and a litter box. I was scared, unsure of the future. I was worried about his reaction and whether he would be able to find me (I moved a couple of towns away). I was alone, really alone, for the first time. (My entire family lives on the other side of the country.) I think I cried, alone on the air mattress that night. But at the same time, I had never felt so FREE. That night and the days to follow helped me become ME again. I felt better than I had in years.

It was an incredible feeling that is nearly impossible to describe. I try to relive – and live in – that perspective every day now. If I ever feel inadequate or find myself making unnecessary concessions to other people, I try to bring myself back to that feeling of freedom and free will. I remind myself that I am an autonomous, unique being who does not have to submit to anyone. It seems crazy that I had to go through what I did to find this confidence in myself, but in some ways I'm glad that I did, because this feeling, this indestructible belief in my capabilities, will never go away. I will never again find myself in a situation like that. It is perhaps the one good thing that came out of that relationship.

As to any advice I might have: Don't blame yourself. You are not crazy, and you don't deserve that kind of treatment. Remember that you have it within you to make drastic changes, even if they seem big or scary or impossible. Be confident and proud of who you are. You have the ability to change your reality. I think that, at least for me, the most important part of healing was stepping away from the source, speaking honestly and openly about the experience, and having reassurance from others that I did the right thing.

**

12

MY HANSEL AND GRETEL LIFE

This chapter presents two stories that illustrate some of the themes described in the last chapter: the exploitation of religion, a preoccupation with sex in voyeuristic and sadistic ways (more fully illustrated in the next chapter), intrusiveness, manipulation, shaming efforts, diminishment, etc.

This chapter and the next illustrate different aspects of an authoritarian's preoccupation with sex. An authoritarian's aggressiveness is regularly tinged with sexual sadism and his or her intrusiveness is often voyeuristic in nature. In the classical literature on the authoritarian personality, this obsession with the sexual (and bathroom) activities of others is given a Freudian interpretation. Whatever its causes, you can expect that your client will have had to deal with this aspect of the authoritarian personality, either personally or as a witness to the abusive and intrusive treatment of other family members.

Here is the first example, Anne's story.

* *

My mom was the authoritarian I had to deal with. While her authoritarian personality didn't emerge until I was in puberty, it had a pervasive effect on my life.

My older sister was openly defiant and became destructively rebellious over time. I remember my sister screaming when my mother held her hands over hot burners to teach her not to steal. I also remember that my sister would simply toss her sanitary napkins in the bathroom trash can; so as to teach my sister a lesson, mom made a soup out of some gathered, used bloody napkins and forced her to eat some of that soup.

I responded by being the most compliant, respectful girl. I was terrified of what I was witnessing. I buried myself in schoolwork, reading, and would have secretive nighttime revelries polishing off a large chocolate bar listening to music in the dark. I became a chubby preteen, and my mother took this development and ran with it. She would apologize for her outbursts of anger by conspiring with me and consulting with me on which cake she should bake for the family (my favorites of course) and giving me extra servings of dinner because I was a "growing girl."

I look back now and feel like I was in Hansel and Gretel, getting fattened up for future slaughter. This future became one of humiliation, taunting, and seeking solace outside the home in blessed fortunate situations where I would encounter healthier supportive surrogate parenting.

My mom was definitely an authoritarian leader type. She became shop steward at the factory she worked in. She was assertive and my dad was passive. Much later in life, I discovered she had threatened to withhold any intimacy with my father unless he was compliant with beating my sister. He would weep and apologize to my sister while having her tied and flogged.

Between her own harsh history as the daughter of an immigrant mid-European family, not having adequate resources to more healthfully respond to my sister's defiance, and probably untreated depression and rage, this behavior was cultivated over time, I think. I believe it started out as a parenting style that then became a pervasive personality trait.

The result is that I have become damaged goods. One snapshot of the damage was going to my grandmother's funeral, knowing that my mother would be there. I begged my then-husband to not move from his position in the church pew between me and my mother. I felt that if my mother turned around and looked at me, I would be psychically incinerated. I was terrified.

I had successfully separately myself from some of the vulnerability by the sheer will of walking out with the clothes on my back and carefully crafting a life. It was a fragile shell of normality at first. I was shocked that my then-husband just smirked and changed his position in the pew on purpose, knowing how scared I was. I became so furious it became the undoing of our marriage.

I am blessed to have had much love and support dealing with the aftermath of being witness to horrors and the terrified one surviving horrific times. My ex had told me that in relaying what he knew of the whole story to some experts, those experts told him that unless I was able to confront my mother, I would never be whole. Thank God that I had support, including the support of a therapist, and eventually I called my mother to reconnect. She was bitter and venomous, complaining that my sister had been such a bad seed.

Right then I made my first ultimatum ever to my mom, indicating that she could choose to take down my phone number or we could disconnect. She got a pencil and paper. There is a long story to tell about that rocky road of reconciling with a difficult mother. Let it be said that when driving to the family house even after the first time back, I had to pull over to the side of the street and retch because it was so overwhelming. I should mention that the first time I visited the house, my mother came to the front door holding the collar of their Doberman/Shepard, who was snarling and snapping. My mother commanded, "Sic her," and let go of the collar. Seriously.

All of this has been addressed in therapy, and that has been helpful. I've received depression and anxiety diagnoses; I'm a pack rat; I'm an overeater. Yes, I'm sure there's a direct correlation between all these disorders and being wounded by my mother. I know that I also had my own personal PTSD when I first left home; that was wretched.

At first, I failed miserably at college, and I am a smart, capable woman. I would experience flashbacks that mom was coming to get me with the police to bring me back home. I'm remembering now that the first time I ran away from home during the course of a miserable weekend, when I came back home my younger sister physically blocked me from leaving the house again. She had no idea what had transpired in my life and just saw me as being hurtful to my parents. She had such a different picture of the family!

I still have issues with anger. I freeze. I have been terrified that being angry myself would unleash destructive forces. I am still learning about healthy expressions of anger. As to any advice I have to give, it would be the following. Don't blame yourself. Give yourself time and allow people to love you. You will make mistakes along the way – love yourself anyway. Seek help when you are open to it. Life can be enjoyable and you don't have to be in misery. This takes time – in many ways a lifetime. May your healing be a gift that you share with others. I was devastated to be disowned from the family will but perhaps I have the best inheritance ever, though: I am intact and I am living my life.

* *

In Maria's story, which follows, her mother is a classic aggressive authoritarian and her husband's authoritarian nature is less pronounced, not clearly emerging until the birth of their child and seemingly more reactive than aggressive. Still, even if he looks less aggressive and less exploitative now, we may suppose that this will change and worsen as his daughter grows – and hits puberty. What is now just meanness over her infant daughter's desire to take her sunglasses along with her from the car may well escalate as she moves into adolescence and puberty and into her sexuality. Doesn't that escalation seem safe to predict?

It's also worth noting how Maria's mother exploits religion as a way to fuel her hatred. Given that she wishes that everyone was a Christian, and given that billions of people aren't, she has provided herself with an endless supply of people to chastise, castigate, and hate. This is such a simple way to create enemies! First, say that everyone should believe what you believe. Then, hate them when they don't. No dynamic is more central to the authoritarian personality than this one.

* *

My mother neglected me emotionally. When I was about four or five years old, I became scared of her. Her method of discipline was to take her anger out on me physically, by spanking me with a belt. Naturally, I'd cry from the pain, and then she'd yell at me to stop crying or she'd really give me something about which to cry, which only induced more tears from fear of being spanked again. Spanking was the discipline of choice for every infraction, no matter how minor.

When she was angry about something else, I'd hide or go to my room and clean it so that if she found me, my behavior would hopefully be pleasing so that she wouldn't turn her anger on me. I learned quickly that avoiding her presence and behaving as pleasing as possible toward her when she was present was my best defense. I'd hide in a tree on our large property with a good book and be safe from her until I had to return home for food. During the summers, I'd tag along with my father on every possible errand (he was self-employed), simply because it got me away from my mother. She has since apologized multiple times for the way she raised me, but the words aren't enough.

With my husband, his authoritarian side didn't really appear until we had a daughter. I first noticed it after we had bought a pair of sunglasses for our nine-month-old daughter, who loved them, and he insisted that she leave them in the car when we got home. He didn't care that she was only nine months old and was very possessive of her new glasses. He wanted her to learn that she needed to leave sunglasses in the car. To this day he is always ready – and sometimes seems anxious – to punish her for her misbehavior instead of teaching her how to behave.

I believe my mother is an authoritarian leader and authoritarian through and through because she wants to impose her will on the rest of the world. As an adult, I've come to find she is staunchly conservative and strict about rules (especially morals), to the point of getting angry that newspapers don't publish why a committed crime is wrong when they report it. She laments the deterioration of society's morals and left me stunned when she told me that she believes Christianity to be the best religion for everyone and that everyone should be a Christian. Of course, she has a very limited view of what constitutes a Christian and is rather judgmental of others.

I suspect my husband is more a follower, mimicking how his father raised him. When our daughter falls, he dismisses her pain and crying with "It's okay," or "Shake it off," ignoring whether she is honestly hurt. When my husband is relaxed, he is very playful and active with our daughter in a loving, positive way.

He's patient and corrects with instruction, rather than yelling or punishing. But when he's stressed, his default parenting style is authoritarian and he demands immediate obedience to his commands.

I believe that my mother has a fully authoritarian personality. She has repeatedly given me unsolicited instruction about my marriage from her perspective and honestly expects me to obey her. She pursued a degree in social work late in life and was sadly fired from her first job as a social worker, because the clients didn't feel comfortable with her. I suspect that she instructed them about how to solve their problems as she perceived them and expected them to obey her in the same manner she instructed me on my marriage. She was angry that the clients didn't have to confront her face to face and believed they should be required to tell her directly why they didn't want her as their social worker. She never pursued another job in that field.

I think my husband is adopting an authoritarian parenting style by default because of his father's example. He wants to be a loving, authoritative parent and struggles to achieve this, but it's hard to pave a new road from the only one you've traveled yourself. As to the consequences of all this on me, I suppress my emotions very well, to the point that I often don't understand why I am anxious or why I'm crying excessively at a Hallmark commercial. When I get angry, I suppress it because I was spanked when I expressed anger as a child. When my husband exhibits the same authoritarian parenting that my mother did, I get anxious and angry inside, and when I interfere with his parenting, we get into big fights that chip away at our marriage bond.

I do not love my mother. I have a superficial relationship with her and I take care of her finances now that she lives in a nursing home, but I'm not interested in keeping tokens or pictures of her to remind me of her. I've been in therapy to reconcile the fact that I didn't feel loved by my mother. The therapy didn't really address the authoritarian aspects of my life in those exact words but we have looked at the emotional suppression with which I struggle. I wouldn't say that therapy has helped me in dealing with authoritarian personalities, because I still struggle with my husband's authoritarian parenting. I might look for more therapy.

My mother is likely going to die in the next five years because of her health. At this time, the thought of her death does not make me sad, but I suspect that a lot of feelings of loss may surface at her death, because underneath it all, I've wanted to feel loved by her, and once she's dead, that will be beyond reach. Right now, I avoid my mother as much as possible and just try to be as amiable as I can be when I am around her. I wouldn't say that any of this is finished yet, either with my mother or with my husband.

* *

13

THE NARCISSISM CLUSTER

Narcissism is actually quite a complicated concept, since healthy narcissism is a developmental goal. Human beings ought to take themselves seriously, maintain a strong self-concept and a healthy ego, care about their self-interest and their goals and aspirations, and in these and others ways be "for themselves." Then there's unhealthy narcissism. That's taking self-love to the extremes of grandiosity, arrogance, and selfishness. Narcissism per se is not a negative; at the extremes to which authoritarians take it, it most certainly is.

In previous chapters, we've looked at an aggression cluster of traits and qualities and an exploitation cluster of traits and qualities. I've also described what I consider to be the authoritarian's prime agenda, a hate-and-punish agenda. If we tie some of these threads together and hazard some guesses, it's easy and logical enough to suppose that an authoritarian is someone who hates because he feels deeply injured, who as a result wants others injured, and whose narcissism is not real self-love or real self-admiration but actually a defense against feeling small, injured, and inferior. I personally find this vision compelling. Whether or not it's the correct explanation, what we know for certain is that authoritarians manifest the following 12 qualities and traits of the unhealthy narcissist. Their victims say that they do.

Grandiosity and Egotism

Whether or not authoritarians actually believe that they are special and superior, they behave as if they are. It is a bit of typical authoritarian grandiosity to believe that they caused an event to happen which in fact had multiple causes and which any right-thinking person would only take partial credit for, to believe that their contributions to a project were invaluable even if they were only marginal, and to take the spotlight and point it at themselves when it is someone else's event or occasion.

Respondent Zachary explained,

> When my sister got married, my father gave the most amazing wedding speech – and he wasn't drunk and delivering something off-the-cuff, it was all prepared. First, he managed to ridicule the groom. Then he managed to ridicule my sister. Then, amazingly, he started promoting his legal services – his divorce services! People actually gasped and my uncle (on my mother's side) had to be restrained from going up there and throwing a punch. The thing that no one could understand was, "Why?" Why do that? Why ruin your daughter's wedding? There was just no scenario where what he did made any sense.

Paranoia and Enemies' Lists

Authoritarians, in part to explain to themselves their bottomless reservoir of hate, act as if they're being continually threatened and endangered. They see enemies everywhere, including (and often especially) in former friends. As respondent Emily put it,

> My older brother kept an actual enemies' list in high school. It went with his tight, rigid personality, his anger, and the way he never fit in anywhere. He was so uncomfortable, awkward and off-putting that naturally all the other kids wanted nothing to do with him – they gave him a wide berth and so they got added to his enemies' list. He spent most of his time plotting his revenge on them.

Truth Held as Enemy

Authoritarians have little regard for the truth. If your agenda is to punish others because you are filled with hatred and anger, the truth of any particular matter is a mere inconvenience. As respondent Phillip put it,

> My father, a pastor, baldly lied about everything, from the number of people who attended one of his church services, a number he always inflated, to the crime rate in the 'bad part of town,' a number he likewise always inflated. It took me years to understand that every lie came from the same place: the place of making himself look better and others look worse. Then he could pat himself on the back and feel smug and superior.

Unacknowledged Anxiety

Some significant percentage of an authoritarian's rigidity and need to control others is caused by his or her unacknowledged anxiety. Robert Altemeyer's research into "right-wing authoritarianism" suggests just how many religious authoritarians have an unconscious and unacknowledged fear that their god does not exist and consequent anxiety connected to that powerful fear. As respondent Leslie put it,

> To the world, my authoritarian brother looks like the least anxious person on the planet. But I know better. To take one example, he couldn't travel on a special trip to Europe with his wrestling team because he was in a panic about flying. But he couldn't admit his fear and had to make up some preposterous story to get out of that trip. I don't think anyone ever knew that it was all about anxiety. By the way, he hasn't gotten to Europe yet.

Superstitions and Mythic Determination

Much of the hatred that authoritarians feel connects to their belief that this life has failed them and betrayed them. They deserved more; they expected more; they were entitled to more. The pain of this thwarted narcissistic entitlement is reduced by belief in a mythical future time when they will get their just rewards and their enemies will get their final punishment. As respondent Henry explained,

My father loved that song "Tomorrow Belongs to Me" from Cabaret, where that angelic Hitler youth sings to enthralled German beer drinkers. He also seemed magnetically pulled to every sort of occult thing, from astrology to the Tarot to you-name-it. He took that all seriously and saw signs and portends everywhere, especially about calamities and disasters for other people – which thrilled him.

Demands and Coercion

Authoritarians make demands as a matter of course and will do everything in their power, including using coercive means, to force you to meet those demands. Their efforts at coercion can include emotional blackmail, threats of violence, threats of abandonment, and threats of reprisal, especially from an angry god. As respondent Anna remembered,

> My mother, who considered me an evil and disobedient girl, continually tried to scare me with her religious notions. Even when it came to something like washing the floor, god got into it – he was going to punish me in the most horrible ways if I didn't get the floor washed perfectly. My sister, who was just like my mother, would jump in with her false piety and echo everything my mother said. They were like two witches – or two jackals.

Need for Domination

Authoritarians feel a powerful need to dominate others. This is true whether they are more an authoritarian follower and passive in certain areas of their life or more an authoritarian leader and hungry for complete domination. As respond Emily put it,

> My sister had to be the center of attention all the time. She loved to make fun of others, put the weak or the disabled down, make herself feel more important, and dominate every situation. From childhood, I knew this was wrong. Her behavior never stopped – throughout our lives she continued belittling others, pumping herself up and, like the vulture

she was, soaring down and making mincemeat out of her "prey." She ran for many offices and won, too, including becoming the mayor of her town (several times). She lived for power and control – all with a touch of sadism.

Lack of Conscience and Absence of Guilt

Many interesting experiments in social psychology, experiments that have been replicated across cultures, socioeconomic classes, and genders with the same results, demonstrate the extent to which a majority of people lack a conscience and feel little guilt. It therefore isn't surprising that authoritarians, given their hate-and-punish agenda, appear devoid of conscience and, having acted despicably, feel no subsequent guilt. When Hannah Arendt (in her book *Eichmann in Jerusalem*) coined her now-famous phrase "the banality of evil" to describe Adolph Eichmann and, by extension, other fascist leaders and followers, she likely meant to convey this particular aspect of their personality: that the evil they perpetrate is internally undramatic and produces no roiling inner conflicts, since they have no conscience or guilty feelings with which to contend.

Lack of Compassion and Empathy

If an authoritarian's agenda is hatred-and-punishment, it will not serve him to access his compassion, empathy, or humanity. It isn't that he doesn't possess these qualities or skills – indeed, he may act very compassionately toward his dog or, as a conman, have honed his empathic skills beautifully. Rather, they don't connect to or serve his central agenda. As respondent Mark explained,

> When a coworker of mine explained to our (very authoritarian) boss that he needed to leave early on a Friday because his wife was having a medical procedure, my boss replied, "You're not having the procedure, are you?" It was in a way – in a horrible way – fascinating how consistent he was in his

lack of compassion toward everyone. You could absolutely count on him not caring.

Conventionalism, Social Status, and Superficial Charm

One of the most robust findings across all of the authoritarian literature is the extent to which authoritarians are conventional in their thinking and intensely concerned with their social status and with looking good to others. Because of their concern with looking good, they regularly appear charming and charismatic. You would not mistake most authoritarians for charm school graduates but a certain percentage manifest a calculated narcissistic charm, especially in social situations and especially around strangers.

Respondent Ellen explained,

> My brother was obsessed with his appearance – in all senses of the word. He was a real dandy, which was a pretty absurd look in our working-class neighborhood. He cared about how he smelled and was always worried about whether he looked or smelled sweaty. And behind all that sweet-smelling façade was someone who tyrannized my sister and me. In public, we were his darling sisters and he could charm people with his stories about how cute we were. In private he hurt us badly.

Submissiveness and Cowardice

In the authoritarian literature, there is a sharp distinction made between authoritarian leaders and authoritarian followers. Both are authoritarians; but they have their significant differences. One major difference is that authoritarian followers, for all their hatred, belligerence, and aggressiveness, are also highly submissive, easily cowed by authority, and cowardly. As respondent Susan explained,

> My mother was authoritarian but more of a follower than a leader, although she liked to present herself as strong and independent. When it came time to prove herself and her strength, she never followed through and always submitted to

the opinions of others. She was terribly concerned with doing things "right" and cared much more for what others, especially those she considered authorities, thought than what anyone in the family thought or felt. She was never on our side.

Loyalty Demands

Authoritarians, though disloyal themselves, demand loyalty from those around them. "Loyalty" in this context translates as "the only principle is me." Respondents repeatedly report that the authoritarian in their life, without making the slightest effort to earn it, demanded their unqualified loyalty, even if that included lying and endangering themselves. Respondent Max recalled,

> My older brother stole a car. When he got caught, he demanded that I tell the police that I stole it. He took me by the shoulder and said, "'That's what a younger brother does for an older brother." He actually had the gall to say, "You know, nothing matters more than loyalty." I looked him in the eye and said "No freaking way." We haven't spoken since."

In the mental disorder universe, the following are some of the criteria for warranting a narcissistic personality disorder. You exaggerate your own importance. You're preoccupied with fantasies of success, power, beauty, intelligence, or ideal romance. You require constant attention and admiration from others. You are envious of others and believe that others are envious of you. You exploit others to reach your goals. You have unreasonable expectations of always being treated well. You believe that you're special and that you can only be understood by other special people. And you disregard the feelings of others. Think of how your client must have fared, given his or her contact with this sort of person.

And think of how your client is likely to be with you. Here is Madeline on her relationship to therapy:

> I never really benefitted from therapy because I was never really there. On the one hand, I was always there – punctual,

obliging, and agreeable. If my therapist made a suggestion I always agreed with it. If my therapist wasn't the sort to make suggestions, I would just talk and talk, often just repeating myself. As much as I was there, I really wasn't there at all. Even when I said something insightful, something that surprised me by its wisdom, I didn't take it in, because the whole thing was just me being agreeable. I never did any work outside of session; and then after a while I would find a reason to switch therapists – maybe I suspected that the current one was getting on to me.

In the next chapter we look at what seems to be a paradox or contradiction: why do narcissistic authoritarians, who portray themselves as superior and above everyone else, care so much about what other people think of them? Let's look at that next.

14

NARCISSISM, CONVENTIONALITY, AND PASSIVITY

How do unhealthy narcissism, conventionality, passivity, and a need for social approval possibly hang together? If I am a preening, selfish, egotistical individual who feels himself to be special, why would I care what others think, pay so much attention to matters of status and social class, and worry whether I'm looking good or toeing a conventional line? Isn't there something contradictory in me feeling like a god and then caring so much what mere mortals think about me?

There have been many psychological explanations proposed to help explain this conundrum. One way that appeals to me is to imagine the following possible connection. If I actually feel small rather than large and if my narcissism is more a cover for feelings of inferiority rather than anything like genuine self-confidence, self-respect, or self-approval, then it would make sense that I would display my small, scared self in many situations, especially with regard to strong leaders, thus leading to passivity, and that I would desperately desire not to be exposed as small, weak, or ruined, which exposure might result from me acting in unconventional ways or stepping out of line. Thus my "hollow" narcissism might lead in a direct line to passivity and conventionality.

If something like this is going on inside of authoritarians, and especially inside of authoritarian followers, then, in addition to their reservoir of hatred and their burning need to punish, we have a third core element to consider: a hollowness, a smallness, and a sense of personal ruination that leads directly to passivity, conventionality, and submissiveness. Thus, the authoritarian agenda I set out earlier, that hate-and-punish agenda, may more properly be thought of as a hate-punish-and-conceal agenda. It is a certain hollowness, emptiness, and smallness that is being concealed and that leads to maneuvers like deception, duplicity, secrecy, and manipulation.

Let me add the following in passing. An additional consideration to touch upon is the possibility that passive, conventional, narcissistic authoritarians are not quite smart enough to be active, instrumental, and unconventional. Consider Josef Smolik's observations in "The Influence of the Concept of Authoritarian Personality Today" (in *Central European Political Studies Review*):

> A large-scale research study undertaken from 1970–1985 in the Netherlands by J. D. Meloen and C. P. Middentorp has shown the strongest negative correlation between authoritarianism and the level of education of the respondent and his father. Other, more general studies have shown that authoritarianism correlates not so much with the level of education as with intelligence. The authoritarian personality is simply less intelligent. Authoritarianism is a consequence of the level of achieved learning and an inability to cognize. Troubles connected with understanding a complicated reality lead to a situation in which people invoke opinions and instruction of authorities, and employ simplified, black-and-white categories of thought.
>
> (Balík, Kubát 2004)

In addition to the various psychological explanations and to the so-to-speak cognitive or capacity explanations I just mentioned, there are also quite plausible existential explanations. I find the existential explanation that authoritarian submissiveness, conventionality, and passivity are "flights from freedom" and flights from personal efficacy and responsibility to be compelling parts to the puzzle. Smolik explained:

> Fromm considered authoritarianism to be one of the possible mechanisms which allow the individual to evade freedom, and defined this phenomenon as "a tendency to surrender the independence of one's own individual ego, to merge it with someone or something outside oneself and thus gain a

force which is absent from his own ego." Submission to an authority means transferring responsibility to another and is "an expression of the inability of the individual ego to live on its own," because "the drive for power does not root in force but in weakness. It is a desperate attempt to obtain a secondary force where true force is missing" and a consequence of "the conviction that life is determined by forces outside the person itself, outside his interests and wishes."

In whatever ways that an authoritarian's particular passivity and particular conventionality ought to be conceptualized, they are no doubt wrapped up with his or her unhealthy narcissism. Healthy narcissism, as developmental psychologists conceptualize it, is a personality plus where a strong sense of self leads to and allows for intimate, reciprocal relationships, empathy, individuality, and an acceptance of the requirements of freedom. The unhealthy narcissism of the authoritarian, by contrast, made up as it is of false self-confidence, a sense of emptiness and hollowness, and defensive grandiosity, lead to conventionality, submissiveness, and passivity.

How does this aspect of the authoritarian personality play itself out in the lives of your clients who have been wounded by authoritarian contact? Respondent Priscilla explained:

When I think of authoritarian personalities the person that always comes up for me is my uncle, my mother's younger brother. There is also an imaginary person, someone who stems from growing up in post-Holocaust Germany. It is a faceless SS officer in uniform and boots – it's all about the boots.

With regard to my uncle, I always felt uncomfortable around him and very, very judged. He was a high school teacher and then later principal. He and his wife felt like the epitome of enforced normalcy, with their oppressive assumption that "everyone" knows what's done and what isn't, and that it was necessary to pooh-pooh and crowd out everything and everyone that wasn't normal.

My parents were anything but normal, and I didn't feel normal at all. There was something sharp, acrid, and poisonous in this insistence on my uncle's part as to what was normal, and I feel that oppression to this day (I am in my early 60s.) Whenever my fear of not being accepted comes up, the specter of my uncle and his wife show up. And when the fear intensifies, the SS officer shows up.

My mother and he had a falling-out that lasted for quite a few years because he felt she was not behaving appropriately when she was a young woman. Then she married my father, an artist who was struggling with mental illness and addiction, which prompted him to turn his concern with normalcy on my father. After my mother died, I saw the letter he had written to her on the occasion of my father's death, lamenting all the terrible situations my father had gotten my mother into, when he (my uncle) knew full well how much my mother loved my father.

It was so tactless and hurtful, right after my father's death. Again, it felt like he needed to make clear who gets to be normal and therefore accepted in some imaginary circle and who didn't. His is the image that I see when my differentness feels like the reason I don't fit in (at work, for example), but at the same time it has made me a passionate fighter for inclusivity.

Respondent Robert explained:

It's very hard to get at what made my father tick. For me, it came down to him just not being as bright as my mother, who was smart, educated, and loved to think about things. My father was very working class and it felt as if at some point he decided to take pride in being uneducated and to take "smart" as a dirty word. He was always saying, "How smart of you!" just before he smacked you. If you had an idea about anything – even the smallest thing – you were pretty much asking for a beating.

I've tried to make sense of his attitudes and positions and they hung together in some strange way that I can intuit but not explain. For instance, I understood intuitively that to say anything against the football team and the basketball team he rooted for was experienced by him as the height of disloyalty.

You couldn't even joke about a missed free throw! There was something going on inside of him where identifying with his teams almost was his personality. The same with identifying with our town, which he didn't even like – if you came in to shop from the next town, you were somehow the enemy. It was all to make himself feel bigger and better – we have the best teams, we have the best town, we have the best religion, we have the best country, feelings that he held with a vise grip.

At the same time, there was this very, very strange passivity going on in him. Even if he had the strongest opinion in the world, and even if it was a matter of real importance to him, he would never voice that opinion in public. There was a time where there was this zoning committee meeting where the outcome of the meeting would significantly affect my father's business. He went to the meeting and took us all with him as some sort of show of force. But even though he had all of these things that he was going to say, when the time came he said nothing. When he got home he exploded and destroyed an old wooden chair by smashing it against a wall. We all hid. We had never seen him that furious and out of control. You just knew it was about his failure to speak up at the meeting – somehow the bluster and the bravado before, the not speaking up in the moment, and the fury afterward all made a certain kind of sense.

Respondent Lois experienced one particular significant consequence as a result of growing up with a passive, conventional, narcissistic authoritarian mother: three children by the time she was twenty. Lois explained:

My mother was like that character in the Dickens novel who would knit and gossip in the front row at the foot of the guillotine while French aristocrats were having their heads chopped off. She was a completely conventional, gossipy, socially conscious, angry, hateful woman. She was beyond prejudiced and would say things about Jews, blacks, Latinos, and just about every group not exactly like her that would make your hair stand on end. But it would all be so quiet, so mild-mannered, so proper, that it almost – just almost – seemed benign. And if you dared disagree with her, all the light went out of her eyes and she would go to a very dark place.

I could feel inside of me how this was going to play out, that I was going to rebel in some really self-sabotaging, destructive way. But I also knew that I didn't have a ghost of a chance of preventing that acting out. I could feel myself hurtling down a road at a hundred miles an hour, spurred on or fueled on by my mother's quiet, mild-mannered, horrible voice. So, what did I actually do? I hooked up with an African-American boy, stayed with him on and off for four years – he was always leaving, coming back, and leaving again – and had three children with him. I don't want to call having my children self-destructive, but I don't think I was operating with free will – I was really somehow "getting even" with my mother.

Respondent Maria explained:

It's funny to call my older brother an authoritarian or a narcissist but I know he's both. He went down the strangest path – well, maybe not so strange, given how religious a family we grew up in. He decided early on that he would serve God as a clergyman and he started wearing this smile, like he knew everything and that he was just indulging you in whatever you were thinking. He never actively did anything, he was the most passive person you've ever met, he was always receiving, receiving, receiving, receiving a new message from on high, either literally or figuratively, and so you could never really talk to him. He had the most incredible self-disciplinary rules and the most conventional opinions about everything. But I could see shining through all of this a particular kind of narcissism – he was anointed and knew that he was in a better position vis-à-vis God than you were.

Here's how his narcissism would play itself out. He once refused to get on a plane because God told him that this plane was going down. I thought it was the height of narcissism for him to believe that God would single him out for sparing – that he was the only worthy one getting aboard that plane and the only one God felt like reaching out to. The whole idea that God would destroy a plane with hundreds of passengers on it just to punish them and that God had gathered hundreds of sinners together to punish them all at once just struck me as nutty. What could the children on the plane have been guilty of? But my brother believed that he had been personally spared and that the others had been personally condemned. That the plane didn't actually crash made zero difference to him in his way of thinking.

But it was an odd narcissism, after all, because he also hated himself. He tried to kill himself more than once. Even his suicide attempts were passive, taking pills but not quite enough pills, but they were still real attempts or at least came from a real place of despair and self-loathing. I don't know how his strictness, his close-mindedness, his self-inflation, and his self-hatred all hung together, but I'm positive that's all inside him, making him look to the world like the mildest, least aggressive, most passive person you could ever want to meet while masking some wild hatreds and real self-loathing.

Each of your clients will have reacted to this narcissism, passivity, and conventionality triad in his or her own way. Some will mirror it and present with a history of passivity and conventionality. Others will have reacted with impulsivity, recklessness, and antiauthoritarian and maybe antisocial behaviors. The headline is that when your client describes a family member or other close contact whose behaviors do not sound overtly authoritarian or clearly narcissistic, but instead sound like the soul of passivity and conventionality, you may still be looking at authoritarian wounding. If you have a hunch that such may be the case, it may prove worthwhile to inquire.

15

KILLING THE FAMILY DOG

We see many of the features of the narcissism cluster – a concern with social status and a lack of empathy, compassion, conscience, and guilt among them – in Vivien's story, which includes an account of her father's bizarre euthanasia of the family pet.

Vivien also asks a fascinating question at the end: did she and her sisters get along so well because they genuinely loved each other or because they had been so well trained in never asserting themselves and never asking for what they wanted and needed?

When an authoritarian's narcissism prevents you from growing a full self, can you even tell if you have the ability to love? This is another harrowing result of authoritarian wounding. Here is Vivien's story.

* *

My father was a true authoritarian in all of his roles in life: as father, husband, brother, employee, boss, neighbor, and friend. He had four daughters and no sons to raise and parent and no emotion was ever allowed. I remember being eight years old and eating dinner through my tears because my cat had been killed by a car. My father exploded and slammed his silverware down and sent me to my room because he couldn't eat while I was sitting there obviously upset.

Whenever we asked our father for permission to play at a friend's house or to go to the movies, my father would say no, and then add, "If you ask me again, you will be grounded." Because of this, my sisters and I learned the art of negotiating ("I'll do extra chores if I can play with my friends later") and feared asking for anything. That fear of asking for anything has extended into adulthood. It is difficult to ask my spouse for help or my boss for a day off. I am always poised for an explosion or for a rant of reasons why I do not deserve these things.

If we visited anyone with our father, my sisters and I were warned to "sit quietly and don't do anything to embarrass me." As adults, when my sisters and I were sitting with the pastor planning my mother's funeral, the pastor noted how we all sat so quietly and in our birth order. We hadn't noticed until then that whenever my sisters and I gather in a room and sit around a table, we sit in our birth order as we were taught as children.

When my sisters and I played when we were little, we were often reprimanded for giggling. When my children were young, I could never get enough of the sound of their laughter. We were never allowed to join sports or other organizations if it meant that my parents would have to drive us somewhere, because my father worked all day and he was not about to "cart around his children" all night. Later in life, when I sought therapy for a marital problem, one of the first questions my therapist asked was "Which parent was the alcoholic?" Neither of my parents drank, but the stories of childhood and my reaction to them was similar to those people who had an alcoholic parent.

Most people who knew my dad said that they were afraid of him. Adults never questioned or challenged him in any way. My father had very firm beliefs about how things should be, and he was always very concerned about how others would see him. I somewhat see that as cowardly now, and I am not sure whether I would call him a leader or a follower. But I'm sure that my father's authoritarian personality was "through and through." My mother never worked or learned to drive. My father saw it as his role to support her, and he would drive her anywhere that she needed to go. I now see that as a very cowardly thing to do, to stunt her growth for the sake of his perceived masculinity.

We had a golden retriever that liked to bark when it was outside. One day a neighbor called and asked my father to keep our dog quiet. My father immediately took the dog to the vet to be euthanized and promptly reported that to the complaining neighbor. He was certain that the neighbor would feel like an ass for complaining and that that would teach him a lesson about making my father look like a bad neighbor or a bad pet owner.

The main consequence of all this is that I have very low expectations of others. If I am overlooked at work, I will not inquire about it. More often than not I have been told to "raise the bar" when I am considering what is fair for myself. As a child, if I said, "Boy, it's hot out today," my father would say that I didn't know what hot was until I worked all day on a construction site in the heat like he had. As a result, I have not sought medical care when needed, as I often thought that my symptoms did not warrant it. I had numerous gallbladder attacks and never sought care, until one morning I work up with yellow skin as my gallstones had caused a complete blockage. The doctor was shocked that I had endured the attacks without seeking care. I didn't trust that my level of suffering warranted attention.

Late in my 35-year marriage – that was mostly a happy one – my husband became an alcoholic. As I sought counseling to cope with his disease, I learned a lot about myself, and if I could afford it, I would pursue more of it. I loved learning about myself (the good and the bad) and exploring my way of seeing the world. My father passed away about six months ago and of course his dying process was going to be his way. He was dying of cancer and should have gone into hospice. He insisted on dying at home without any "outsiders" assisting, and of course, all of his "good" daughters turned our worlds upside down to alternate doing the daunting task of caring for him.

I lived two and a half hours away, but took Fridays off and drove down every weekend to do my part. When we tried to speak with him about alternate care, it was shut down, as we knew it would be, and as obedient daughters, we did our part. On the last two days of his life, when he was in and out of consciousness, we arranged for an ambulance ride to hospice as he was too weak to fight us and we didn't have to face him. My sisters and I are all 60 years and older, and his authoritarian grip was as tight as ever right up until his death. We were all very aware, and yet not one of us individually, or as a group, felt we had the power to stand up to him even as he lay weak and dying.

I had been in therapy weekly for about two years to cope with my alcoholic husband (who has since passed). Questions about any authoritarian personalities only came up when my therapist inquired about support among my family. I remember her inquiring as to whether I could seek assistance from my parents when I was considering a divorce. I explained that I could not ask for help. My father would have said that "you made your bed, now you lie in it" or "It's your life, go figure it out."

In the past two years, I lost my mother first and then my father. My sisters and I have spoken often about our childhood, often with laughter when we see how ridiculous our childhood was and how differently we raised our children. Neither of our parents hugged us or told us that they loved us. My sisters and I all expressed our love to my parents when they were dying, and they did reciprocate with an "I love you," but never before that. Christmas cards and birthday cards were simply signed "Mom and Dad." Therapy for dealing with an authoritarian would definitely have been interesting, but just seeing how my sisters and I were still under his authoritarian grip at the end of his life was quite compelling.

I don't believe that my sisters and I have any mental health disorders. I believe we have had productive and happy lives; however, the parental impact is very clear to my sisters and I and has strongly influenced the choices we have made. Moving away from my parents and waiting until much later in life to pursue things that we knew would not be approved of was one way of dealing with our authoritarian father. My sister is a Lutheran pastor who went to school for her Master of Divinity when she was 55 years old. My father never approved because she is divorced and therefore was not deemed good enough to become a spiritual leader.

Limiting contact with my father was definitely helpful. I often visited with my mother when I knew my father was not home. However, the long-lasting impact of having him for a father is ever-present. I was taught never to question authority. I feel as though I tolerated poor medical care from doctors, shoddy workmanship from contractors, and many things that another person would have spoken up about. I am learning, though. My father would confront a contractor about his shoddy work by exploding on him. I am learning polite and respectful ways to ask for what I want and what I expect, and most importantly, I am asking.

I think knowing how and why I approach life is very helpful. I don't hate my father or blame him. I accept him for who he was. Understanding his strengths and weaknesses and how they affect me are vitally important to me. As to any advice, I wish I had advice to give, but I really don't.

I see families where the daughters are the little princesses and I feel sad that I did not have that experience. I see young girls who, when things go wrong, can call home and dad will do anything to help make it right, and I feel sad that I didn't have that. I see families attending ceremonies, plays, concerts, and sporting events with parents cheering on their children, and I feel sad because I didn't have that. I see families at the hospital when their children are born, and I feel sad that I didn't have that.

My accomplishments were not recognized and my sorrows were not validated. That is a large missing link. I am determined not to pass on the legacy. I was a lenient parent who probably overcompensated for what I didn't have. I am fortunate to have three sisters who are my rock. They are the ones I turn to in joy and sorrow. We all get along lovingly, and I believe it is because we learned to lean on each other. We buried our parents and divided up the belongings without even the smallest quarrel. Is that because we were taught not to ask or quarrel or is it because we genuinely love each other? I don't really know.

**

How difficult is it to heal from these early wounds? Respondents as a rule reported some healing – but almost never complete healing. They could especially tell how much distance still remained when they resumed contact with the authoritarian in question. As a rule, that contact triggered them and retraumatized them. Here is Marjorie's story.

**

My mother was the authoritarian in my life. She was physically, mentally, and spiritually abusive to me. I don't think I understood those dynamics and how destabilizing her actions truly were until, as an adult, I was attempting to change my behaviors that weren't serving me anymore. Those early experiences crushed my spirit and my self-esteem, and I've had to work through buckets of shame for most of my life. I've lived with tremendous fear, nervousness, and deep sadness.

She was unable to hear input from others and had her own thoughts on how to do things. So, in some respects I believe she was more of an authoritarian leader. However, she did what she did in the name of the Bible and according to what she was taught about children and how they should behave ("Children should be seen and not heard"; "Spare the rod and spoil the child") and in that sense, she was more of an authoritarian follower, I think.

As to consequences, her way of being made it challenging for me to trust myself or to know myself. Therapy helped, but I'm still dealing with triggers. I am 48 years old, and I thought that much of this had been worked out and integrated. About a year ago my father passed away, and I had to become my mother's primary caregiver as she developed dementia. I have discovered that what is most frightening for me is how I automatically get pulled back into past traumas and the very youngest parts of myself.

There are days her manipulation pulls me right back, and I'm in a full PTSD episode. I'm back in the environment that I worked so hard to change. This is the hardest part for me. When I am away from her energy, for the most part, I do feel safer and calmer. However, she is my mother and I feel a real sense of obligation and responsibility. I oscillate from feeling over-responsible to feeling helpless when I'm in her presence. It's all very draining.

I am really facing all this right now. I've noticed over the past year, I haven't been taking care of myself as well as I had previously. I'm allowing old patterns of behavior to come back, and I think it's because my energy is depleted. I know that self-compassion is crucial, but since I internalized the abuse so well, self-compassion becomes a difficult challenge for me. Without sounding pessimistic, I am not sure if the healing will ever be complete. Lord knows I've done enough recovery work, trainings, schooling, therapy, and self-help reading for ten lifetimes. Healing has become my second full-time job and maybe in some sense has even prevented me from living. All I have ever wanted was to feel a sense of peace, comfort, and well-being in my life. Life is difficult enough, but when you've had very early, preverbal trauma, life is doubly difficult.

* *

16

CONSEQUENCES: DEPRESSION

Authoritarian contact leads to negative consequences. These include lifelong sadness, lifelong anxiety, an outsized craving for substances and behaviors (and also outsized revulsions, like being revolted at the sight of food if mealtimes were humiliating), a damaged self-image, an inability to concentrate or to think clearly, and more. Almost always, sadness is part of the picture: sadness, despair, grief, or some sister darkness such as suicidal thoughts or self-mutilating behaviors.

The current mental disorder paradigm, which transforms reactions to life into medical-sounding conditions, acts as if depression is a disease. We have lost sight of the obvious truth that life can make us despair and that a harsh childhood can build despair into our system. If you work from the premise that what you are looking at is not a medical-sounding affliction but despair, then your aim is to reduce that despair.

One reasonable approach is to help your client make the connection between what he or she experienced and how sad that way of living made him or her feel. As obvious as that sounds, investigations of this sort have been jettisoned in the pill age. Nowadays it is more common to "treat the symptoms of depression" than to help clients understand why they are grieving.

If you do this exploring, will clients make the connection between their experiences and their sadness? Absolutely. Respondents to my Authoritarian Wound Questionnaire easily drew the natural conclusion that life with an authoritarian parent (or authoritarian grandparent or sibling) had made them sad – and continued to make them sad, even long after that authoritarian had died, and even to this day. Here is Joanne's story.

**

The term "authoritarian" equals rigidity and abuse in my mind when it comes to thinking of my mom. Her way was the only way. Irrational meanness, anger, and rage. She seemed to have absolutely no idea that we had the right to our own ideas. Expressing an opinion resulted in getting hit or belittled with sarcasm. Being called names. Being hit when I was four to where I didn't know when she would stop. No patience – when I was an adult she admitted that.

At six I froze as she put my two-year-old brother's head in the toilet when he got pee on the seat. I became pregnant at 18; my boyfriend and I wanted to get married. When we told her, she said "Absolutely not! You will have an abortion!" I didn't have the chutzpah to say screw you, escape her authoritarianism, and run away to get married. Not that it would have been a successful marriage. But I would have made my own choice! The next ten months after the abortion and before I went to art school were hell. The grief was unbelievable, and grief came intermittently for decades. On the top of what I'd grown up with, the grief landed me in my first therapy experience.

I had a boss from hell who was like being around my mother, except he didn't hit me or call me names. He was a very angry person and we butted heads a lot. But I did my best to get around him for my clients in Vocational Rehab; I would make someone eligible and he would nix my decision. The same person would have been approved in another district. So, I would tell the client to contact the head of Vocational Rehab or the governor's ombudsmen office, providing them with the appropriate phone number, but not to tell anyone that I had sent them! It always worked. I knew I was right. I wish I'd been able to get around stuff like that with my mom!

My mom was definitely an authoritarian leader. My dad was definitely a follower. He had absolutely no idea what to do with an alcoholic spouse and could be rigid and mostly benignly negligent, not especially present. His authoritarian attitude came across as decisions that were final with no discussion. What was so weird in our house was that our mom was the one we approached for things that we needed as well as money, because we knew that our dad in his own passive authoritarian way would always say no. We grew up not approaching him. But we could approach the crazy one! If you were to do cardboard cutouts of my parents my dad would be in the background. Our friends gave our mom wide berth because she could go off at any time.

My mom was an authoritarian through and through. I think a great deal of her authoritarian parenting was due to depression, rage, and later, alcoholism. She grew up wounded with her own authoritarian alcoholic parents. Pictures of her from about six years old are so unhappy. Her mother adored her father but knew he had wanted his firstborn to be a boy. Her father was an officer in the service and the son of Norwegian immigrants; he ran away from home at age 15 because his father beat him so much.

My mom didn't really want to be married and she was trapped with three kids born within four years. She once told me that there were some women who weren't meant to be a mother and she was one of them. I certainly concurred with her opinion though I didn't tell her that. The one really peculiar – but truly good – thing that she did was to critique my artwork in a very constructive and supportive way. If only the rest of my life had been like that!

For some reason learning that verbal, physical, mental, and sexual violence cause significant alterations of the brain has brought comfort. My difficulties aren't the result of weakness on my part but on the changes in my brain. This doesn't absolve me from working to heal the erroneous beliefs and actions that keep me in pain. It is an ongoing process. I now know that damage to parts of the brain from abuse creates difficulties regulating emotions.

Research has also shown that children who grow up with verbal abuse have alterations in their auditory cortex. That was an aha moment for me because I have an auditory processing disorder. My slight hearing loss isn't enough to create the problems I have. Someone can tell me something several times and it just bounces off my head until I finally get it.

I can hear them but my brain is blocking my comprehension. I have to ask people to repeat things several times because I don't understand the sounds. I don't catch the start of a conversation until several words down the line. It isn't a weakness on my part but rather the consequence of my ears shutting down to protect myself from her. I'm not stupid. It was a defense. I grew up having no confidence in my ability to trust my intuition, to make choices or be able to disagree, to hold my own in an argument, or to withstand someone's anger.

I get very easily hurt and defensive and feel guilty asking for what I want in the first place in addition to feeling guilty for going after something I want. As a consequence, I came to have a beggar mentality. I have a lot of avoidance behavior and I didn't trust myself. I'm a lot better than I used to be but I still sometimes go along with things even though I really don't want to.

I grew up thinking I wouldn't have a good thing come my way so I had better get what I can now. It's hard for me to delay gratification. I don't always trust my decision while making my paintings, so it's hard to finish them. My favorite part of painting is planning them. Usually the titles come at this stage. But then I remember something or something happens and I go to a very dark place. That something could be very small, even just a noise: for instance, hearing a baby cry makes my stomach twist.

Seeing others shocked by what I grew up with was profound. I wasn't being a whiner! And my mom's behavior really was awful – it wasn't normal! Acknowledgement from friends and therapists who support me and realize how hard it was for me growing up and understanding the resulting wounds has been very healing. Going through abuse can be very lonely.

Therapists help me see my blind spots and erroneous thinking. I've gained confidence by following what I wanted to do, such as going to art school, and doing things that I like and experiencing success. I've been told by more than one person that I'm large in spirit (I'm only four foot ten and ninety-five pounds) or that I sounded taller over the phone. They would never have guessed what I was like when I left home to go to art school. Art school was jail break for me and that was when I began therapy. These days I'm working with mindfulness to keep the trash in my mind at bay. I have a lot of successes these days but the trash is still there.

All of this has come up constantly in therapy. My mom has been the root of so much pain in my life. Therapy has helped a great deal because I blamed myself for being and feeling so inferior. The thing that's been found in research is that with authoritarian parents, criticism outweighs whatever praise they dispense. So, getting some praise from my parents didn't make much of a dent in things.

When I was six I was wishing I was dead and I was diagnosed with depression and began therapy when I went away to art school. We had moved a great deal since my dad was in the service – every year of high school was in a different state. There was no long-term local community or friends that we could look to for support that would buffer the home life. In later years, I've been diagnosed with PTSD after growing up with my mom, who was so angry, so unpredictable, so dismissive. My youngest brother has been diagnosed with PTSD too. It was a relief in a way because it confirmed that her behavior and my resulting problems weren't just in my head.

She'd walk into the room and just start whaling on us. We wouldn't know why. At this point I think that bipolar II is the most appropriate diagnosis for me. And, yes, psychiatric drugs do help me. In 2010, I left the job from hell to preserve my sanity and moved to Salt Lake City. About a month and a half later I ended up in a step-down facility for 11 days after calling the suicide hot line. I couldn't read for a couple of months and spent many days sitting on my third-floor balcony looking at one leaf on a tree, the same leaf from August until October.

In Adult Children of Alcoholics therapy, I came to grieve what I never had – a mother who could be a lot more even-tempered and patient. Rather than a total break I moved away – 1500 miles – as did my brothers. I was always apprehensive when she would call. I'd be relieved when she didn't call me – I just couldn't stand the waiting for or receiving her criticism. But I would also feel guilty.

In her last year between being diagnosed with colon cancer and her death, neither I nor my brothers visited her. One brother and I discussed it – our consensus was that we just weren't comfortable around her, and she wasn't comfortable around us either. She had become close to her stepfamily from her second marriage and they took care of her. I'm sure they thought we were real jerks but they hadn't endured her hateful behavior.

I think the other thing that was a little conflicting was that she did instill in us good values which we could appreciate. She had a strong sense of antiracism –using the 'N' word wasn't tolerated, and this included living in New Orleans LA in the 1960s where the word was everywhere. She had despised the snooty treatment of Jewish girls after WWII at her high school. She struggled in high school but was an avid reader of books and had a love of nature, music, and art.

She could have been a brilliant portrait artist but that went out the window with three kids. With each move, she always found an art supply store to work in and she would gift me with art supplies. I still have a watercolor set she gave me in high school – and I'm 63 now. There were times when I would reach out for some serious help and she would come through in an understanding way. I was grateful and as I grew older I came to feel less conflicted. Perhaps she owed me; perhaps this was part and parcel of who she was.

We all cried at her funeral, but not at our father's. He was in our lives so little. You can't miss what you never had. My youngest brother refused to bring his sons to visit our dad because he felt that dad would pretty much ignore the boys after saying hello. After marrying into a very demonstrative Italian family he didn't want to subject his sons to our dad.

In the past, my husband has been authoritarian in his discussions with me and with jokes at my expense. But two times I called him on it and he stopped. He had no idea that he was that way. When I called him on it I felt like a computer chip had suddenly been dropped into my head. It is so hard for me to stand up for myself and I don't know where the words came from.

As to advice, keep looking for support and help and learn how to heal yourself. Read. Find people to listen to your story – therapists and friends – but don't make that your whole life or you'll drive your friends away! You need them! Drop the need to be perfect that makes you put pressure on yourself when you're working on your painting or writing or whatever you do.

Be curious and follow things that excite and interest you. It will make you feel better and take your mind off the crap you grew up with. This is a lifelong process (sorry!). Develop a mindfulness practice so you can step outside the chaos and not make it you. It's been extremely effective with people who have suffered abuse growing up and it's helped with my lifelong depression.

* *

17

CONSEQUENCES: ANXIETY

Virtually all of the respondents to the Authoritarian Wound Questionnaire reported as one consequence of authoritarian wounding a heightened sense of anxiety.

Of course, anxiety manifests in all sorts of ways. One of my specialties is working with stage fright sufferers. For them, their performance anxiety manifests in exactly those ways that are most likely to prevent them from performing. A violinist will come down with shaky wrists, a singer will lose her top range, and so on. Because anxiety is a feature of our early warning system against danger, it should operate in precisely these ways: it should do a nice job of keeping us out of danger by, for example, making sure that we can't perform.

Anxiety manifests as nausea, confusion, panic attacks, phobic reactions, sweats, forgetfulness, dissociative episodes, chronic worries, unproductive obsessions, impulsivity, powerful compulsions, procrastination, passive-aggressive behaviors, and every manner of physical and mental distress. Your client may not report "anxiety" per se but may instead report some or many of the above sorts of complaints. If you are working with a victim of authoritarian wounding, be on the lookout for these complaints.

Let me present just one characteristic respondent story before providing you with a robust anxiety management menu that you can use in your work with clients. In the following report, you won't hear "anxiety" named as such, not until the end. Yet the fear and hypervigilance that Miriam reports are manifestations of anxiety. Miriam explained:

> My father was very controlling and rigid. He would set the rules of the house, which changed on a daily basis, and then would fail to communicate what those rules were until they were being broken, at which time he would become enraged that the rules were being violated. For instance, dinner needed to be on the table by 5:01, not 4:59 or 5:00. If it was not, it landed on the floor when it was set on the table.
>
> He was not supportive as a parent. He frequently was demeaning, more so for myself as the female than my brother. However, there were times when even my brother was in his sights. He was frequently unpredictable and would display widely disparate mood swings. You learned to keep a healthy distance from him until you figured out his mood on a given day. He had a poor relationship with his own father, who was also extremely rigid. I remember visiting my father's father and he would be wearing a three-piece suit on a Sunday afternoon. I can't imagine that there was much nurturance given to my father as a child.
>
> What I remember the strongest was just how unpredictable everything felt every minute of the day when he was in the home. And the feeling of dread that came with knowing he would be coming home soon. His actions, tone, and demeanor were completely a product of his inner beliefs that it was his way or the highway. As a child, I only experienced him as someone who was hell-bent on exerting full control over me. He was someone that was to be feared and not trusted and definitely someone who you never let your guard down around.
>
> This made me fearful and hypervigilant, as you never knew what to expect from him. It made me want to avoid him rather than turn to him as a parent. Our relationship ended when I was twelve and we coldly coexisted under the same roof for another twelve years before my parents divorced. Looking back on my childhood, I am not sure what I did to manage this situation. I know I wrote a lot

and contemplated suicide. That fear and hypervigilance has been with me all these years: in my work life, where I had a very authoritarian boss, and in all aspects of my life. I am finally taking my power back but the anxiety isn't likely to just go away. It'll be my life's work to deal with it.

In my work with coaching clients, I actively teach anxiety management strategies. You may want to, also. What follows is a robust menu of anxiety management strategies. Which of these might you want to learn more about and incorporate in your helping practice? Or use yourself? I think that, of the many things that a humane helper might want to know, almost nothing is more important than knowing what helps to reduce anxiety and knowing how to communicate that information to a client.

Anxiety mastery requires that a client actually do the work of managing and reducing anxiety. It is not enough to have a refined sense of when you are anxious and why you are anxious: you then must do something about it. Most people who know that they are anxious do not make a sufficient effort to actively reduce their anxiety, opting instead to "white knuckle" life, medicate themselves with antianxiety medication (which can be useful in some circumstances), or make do with alternative medicine approaches (like teas or homeopathic remedies). More than this is required to effectively manage anxiety.

Anxiety management requires a diligent, systematic effort to find techniques that work, especially cognitive ones that retrain neurons to "think differently." You might have clients practice some or several of the following 22 anxiety reduction strategies, learn which ones work best for them, and begin to use the ones that work best. "Knowing about them" is not enough – clients must practice them and then actively employ them.

Here are the 22:

Existential Decisiveness

Indecisiveness about what matters, about whether you personally matter, about whether meaning resides over here or whether it resides over there, and about what constitutes the right life for you breed anxiety. When you tackle these issues directly and become existentially decisive, you become less anxious. The first step in becoming existentially decisive is returning control of meaning to you by asserting – and really believing – that you are in charge of the meaning of your life.

Attitude Choice

You can choose to be made anxious by every new opinion you hear, or you can choose to keep your own counsel. You can choose to be overly vigilant to changes in your environment and overly concerned with small problems, or you can shrug such changes and problems away. You can choose to involve yourself in every controversy, or you can choose to pick your battles and maintain a serene distance from most of life's commotion. You can choose to approach life anxiously, or you can choose to approach it calmly. It is a matter of flipping an internal switch – one that you control (or at least can influence).

Personality Upgrading

Maybe the prospect of getting some bad news makes you anxious. All wound up, you lash out at your mate, eat a ton of potato chips, shut down emotionally, or drive dangerously fast. This is your personality at work. You know that most of the people around you could use a bit of a personality upgrade – well, probably the same is true for you. The more aware you become and the less reactive you become, the less anxious you will feel. A key anxiety-management strategy is identifying changes that you would like to make to your personality and then making them.

Improved Appraising

Incorrectly appraising situations as more important, more dangerous, or more negative than they in fact are raises your anxiety level. Say that you are a writer. If you consider it important what weight of paper you use to print out your manuscripts, you are making yourself anxious. If you hold it as dangerous to send out your fiction without copyrighting it because you're afraid that someone will steal it, you are making yourself anxious. If you consider form rejection letters genuine indictments of your work, every form rejection letter will make you anxious. You can significantly reduce your experience of anxiety by refusing to appraise situations as more important, more dangerous, or more negative than they in fact are.

Anxiety Analysis

Most people are made anxious thinking about anxiety! This dynamic prevents them from analyzing their situation and coming to smart conclusions about what triggers their anxiety and what anxiety-management tools they might want to employ to reduce their experience of anxiety. Once you begin to think calmly about the role of anxiety in your life, you can arrive at real solutions. You engage in this analysis straightforwardly by wondering through what provokes your anxiety and where it manifests the most, by identifying how your thoughts and your behaviors increase your anxiety, and by deciding which anxiety-management tools you are going to commit to practicing and learning.

Lifestyle Support

Your lifestyle supports calmness or it doesn't. When you rush less, create fewer unnecessary pressures and stressors, get sufficient rest and exercise, eat a healthy diet, take time to relax, include love and friendship, and live in balance, you reduce your experience of anxiety. If your style is to always arrive chronically late, to wait until the last minute to meet deadlines, and to live in disorganization, you are manufacturing anxiety. How much harder will it be to deal with the anxiety in your life if your very lifestyle is producing its own magnum of anxiety?

Behavioral Changes

What you actually do when you feel anxious makes a big difference. Behaviors like playing games or watching television for hours quell anxiety but waste vast amounts of your time. Behaviors like smoking cigarettes chemically quell anxiety but increase your health risks. If a ten-minute shower or a twenty-minute walk can do as good a job of reducing your anxiety as watching another hour of golf or smoking another several cigarettes, isn't it the behavior to choose? There are time-wasting, unhealthy, and dispiriting ways to manage anxiety and also efficient, healthy, and uplifting ways to manage anxiety. The specific tactics you use to manage your experience of anxiety matter, as some support your life purposes and others undermine them.

Deep Breathing

The simplest – and a quite powerful – anxiety management technique is deep breathing. By stopping to deeply breathe (five seconds on the inhale, five seconds on the exhale) you stop your racing mind and alert your body to the fact that you wish to be calmer. Begin to incorporate deep breaths into your daily routine, especially when you are about to embark on something that you know usually makes you anxious.

Cognitive Work

Changing the way that you think is probably the most useful and powerful antianxiety strategy. You can do this straightforwardly by (1) noticing what you are saying to yourself; (2) disputing the self-talk that makes you anxious or does not serve you; and (3) substituting more affirmative, positive or useful self-talk. This three-step process really works if you will practice it and commit to it.

Incanting

A variation on strategies eight and nine is to use them together and to "drop" a useful cognition into a deep breath, thinking "half" the thought on the inhale and "half" the thought on the exhale. Incantations that might serve to reduce your experience of anxiety are "I am perfectly calm" or "I trust my resources." Experiment with some short phrases and find one or two that, when dropped into a deep breath, help you quell your anxious feelings.

Physical Relaxation Techniques

Physical relaxation techniques include such simple procedures as rubbing your shoulder and such elaborate procedures as "progressive relaxation techniques" where you slowly relax each part of your body in turn. Doing something physically soothing probably does not amount to a full anxiety management practice but can prove really useful in the moment to help you calm yourself. It is especially useful when used in combination with your cognitive practice.

Mindfulness Techniques

Meditation and other mindfulness practices that help you take charge of your thoughts and get a grip on your mind can prove very useful as part of your anxiety management program. It is not so important to become a practiced "sitter" or to spend long periods of time meditating. What's important is to truly grasp the idea that the contents of your mind make suffering and anxiety and that the better a job you do of releasing those thoughts and replacing them with more affirmative ones, the less you will experience anxiety.

Guided Imagery

Guided imagery is a technique where you guide yourself to calmness by mentally picturing a calming image or a series of images. You might picture yourself on a blanket by the beach, walking by a lake, or swinging on a porch swing. You can use single snapshot images or combine images and end up with the equivalent of a short relaxation film that you play for yourself. The first step is to determine what images actually calm you, by trying out various images, and then, once you've landed on images that have the right calming effect, bring them to mind when you are feeling anxious.

Disidentification Techniques

"Disidentification" is the core idea of the branch of psychotherapy known as psychosynthesis. Rather than attaching too much significance to a passing thought, feeling, worry, or doubt, you remind yourself that you are larger than and different from all the stray, temporal events that seem so important in the moment. You do this disidentifying primarily by watching your language. For example, you stop saying "I'm anxious" (or worse, "I'm an anxious person") and begin to say, "I'm having a passing feeling of anxiety." When something negative happens, instead of saying "I'm ruined" or "I'm finished," you say, "I'm having a passing feeling of pain and disappointment." By making these linguistic changes you fundamentally reduce your experience of anxiety.

Affirmations and Prayers

Affirmations and prayers are simply short cognitions that point your mind in the direction you want it (and you) to go. If you are feeling hatred, which breeds conflict and anxiety, you affirm your desire to love, the availability of love, or some other formulation that turns you in the direction that you want to go and that, by turning you in that direction, reduces your experience of anxiety. By affirming your basic worth, your ability to trust yourself, and your willingness to show up to life, you "talk yourself" into a better frame of mind and as a result feel less anxious.

Ceremonies and Rituals

Creating and using a ceremony or ritual is a simple but powerful way to reduce your experience of anxiety. For many people, lowering the lights, lighting candles, putting on soothing music, and in other ways ceremonially creating a calming environment helps significantly. If you're a creative person, one particularly useful ceremony is one that you create to mark the movement from "ordinary life" to "creating time." You might use an incantation, like "I am completely stopping," in a ritual or ceremonial way to help you move from the rush of everyday life to the quiet of your creative work, repeating it a few times so that you actually do stop, grow quiet, and move calmly and effortlessly into the trance of creative work.

Reorienting Techniques

If your mind starts to focus on some anxiety-producing thought or situation, or if you feel yourself becoming too wary, watchful, and vigilant, all of which are anxiety states, one thing you can do is to consciously turn your attention in another direction and reorient yourself away from your anxious thoughts and toward a more neutral stimulus. For example, if you're a musician, instead of focusing on the audience entering the concert hall, which you know increases your anxiety, you might reorient yourself toward the notices on the bulletin board in the green room and casually glance at them, paying them just enough attention to take your mind off the sounds of the audience arriving but not so much attention that you lose your sense of the music you are about to play.

Preparation Techniques

You can reduce your experience of anxiety by being well prepared for situations that in your experience provoke anxiety in you. If public speaking makes you anxious and you're about to give a talk at work, preparing what you are going to say is the natural thing to do to reduce your experience of anxiety. A great deal of the anxiety we experience is anticipatory anxiety and carefully preparing is the key to reducing our experience of anticipatory anxiety.

Symptom Confrontation Techniques

A rarely used technique, employed mostly in some forms of therapy and by some teachers in the performing arts, symptom confrontation is the idea that by "demanding" that your anxiety symptoms get worse and worse – that your querulous singing voice or jumpy violin bowing wrist get even more shaky – and by actively trying to increase your experience of anxiety, you reach a point where you break through into laughter and a sense of the absurdity of your worries.

Discharge Techniques

Anxiety and stress build up in the body and techniques that vent that stress can prove very useful. One discharge technique that actors sometimes learn to employ to reduce their experience of anxiety before a performance is to "silently scream" – to make the facial gestures that go with uttering a good cleansing scream without actually uttering any sound (which would be inappropriate in most settings). Jumping jacks, pushups, and physical gestures of all sorts can be used to help release the "venom" of stress and anxiety and pass it out of your system.

Pharmaceuticals

Taking antianxiety medication is an option with some pluses and many minuses. The major plus is that a chemical tranquilizer, if it happens to work for you, will create an induced experience of calm. That state of calm can provide you with a crucial respite from your experience of anxiety and allow you to begin trying nonchemical solutions that you might not have felt equal to trying while highly anxious. Among the minuses are the side effects of chemicals, the potential for dependency, and the way they divert us from looking for better solutions.

Recovery Work

You can deal with mild anxiety without having to stop everything and without making anxiety management a daily priority. But if your anxiety is more serious and especially if it permeates your life, affecting your ability to relate, to work, and to live, then you must take your anxiety management efforts very seriously, as seriously as you would take your efforts to recover from despair or from an addiction. One smart way to pay this kind of serious attention is by using addiction recovery ideas – for example, the idea of identifying triggers: those thoughts and situations that trigger anxiety in you. Just as you might "work your program" to stay sober, you work your program to stay calm and centered.

Your clients who have been wounded by an authoritarian are almost certain to have anxiety issues. Help them learn to reduce their experience of anxiety by sharing these techniques with them or in whatever ways you know to help anxious folks. I think this is among your top priorities in working with victims of authoritarian contact.

18

CONSEQUENCES: ADDICTION

A characteristic result of authoritarian wounding is the persistent effort to self-medicate by using certain chemicals and to self-soothe by engaging in certain behaviors. The body's demands and the mind's cravings pull at the wounded victim to drink alcohol, use heroin, gamble on the Internet, engage in risky sexual behaviors, or in some other way create a momentary respite from the lifelong pain that is now embedded in their personality.

We have different ways of naming these behaviors: addiction, substance abuse, compulsivity, etc. Labeling apart, and not withstanding any biological proclivities and predispositions (like high tolerance) or biological changes (like cellular adaption to large quantities of alcohol), we are not looking at "diseases" but habitual responses to pain and trauma.

You are in a position to help your clients deal with these pain responses by practicing your idiosyncratic version of recovery work. In addition to trauma-informed care and existential care, which we'll discuss in detail, you'll want to add recovery-oriented care to your battery of helping orientations. Many of your clients will need precisely this help. Here, as the first of the two stories in this chapter, is Harold's story.

* *

Both of my parents were authoritarian personality types. They were emotionally, mentally, and occasionally physically abusive. They were often cruel toward me when I was still young, often treating me as if I was not wanted and certainly not loved and respected.

I am black and from Alabama. My parents were uneducated laborers. In the segregated south, they would have been authoritarian followers in some ways, because they were working for white supervisors (my father was a janitor; my mother was a domestic) and expected to be subservient to those who employed them. They were to stay in their place and keep to their station in the southern social order.

At home, however, they became authoritarian leaders, though for some reasons they appeared to vent most of those tendencies onto me and not my other three brothers. I don't think all my brothers received authoritarian wounding, though they may have been deprived in other ways. I am certain that I was the primary target of my parents' authoritarian behaviors.

I have always felt that I suffered from some sort of condition and now I would call it authoritarian wounding. I've suffered from chronic anxiety and taken medication for that; I've been diagnosed with depression and PTSD. I suffer from a lack of confidence, though I have accomplished many things I am proud of. I am barely capable of knowing how to receive love and affection, I am socially awkward, and only drinking and using make me feel confident socially.

I struggle with intimate relationships; I often struggle with relating in socially respectful ways with women I don't know; my sense of boundaries between myself and others seems permanently broken. I have no idea how personal boundaries are supposed to work, as I was never allowed to have boundaries growing up. My social skills have never really developed fully, neither has my personality, my emotional intelligence, or my maturity.

Some things have helped. Many have been negative things like drinking and using street drugs. I've also used a lot of LSD and prescribed medications. More positively, I'm helped by Buddhist meditation, listening to Miles Davis, John Coltrane, Debussy, and Stravinsky, trying to perform music (jazz saxophone), writing short stories, studying religious and philosophical traditions, and constantly trying to learn and expand what I know about myself and about being a human being on this earth: stumbling ahead but always stumbling, it seems.

I stopped speaking to my father at some point and did not really speak to him for the last seven to nine years of his life. I made a conscious decision not to speak to him any longer. I felt safer and I'm no longer subjected to emotional abuse. I did not do the same with my mother and have just now realized, as I write this, that I need to make a complete break with her also, so that I can begin to heal myself from the abusive relationship she's had with me all my life but that I haven't realized until now.

I have not made a complete break with her but I did stop giving my mother my telephone number, so she couldn't reach me. I live overseas, so she can't come and visit. She can send me an email and I can decide whether or not I will respond to it (I have just realized that it is my choice whether or not I respond to an email, not hers). I think that I have to do an even better job of setting and maintaining strict and severe boundaries with her, with virtually no contact; only that will protect me from continuing to fear her.

I keep trying to heal myself, find the blind spots, deal with negative self-talk, and figure out what to do with the internalized verbal abuse learned from years of being abused by two authoritarian caregivers. Being abused my entire formative life, I find myself either drawn to, unable to recognize, or simply incapable of protecting myself from authoritarian and abusive personality types as an adult. My ability to analyze social situations and interact with people seems permanently damaged.

I am much better than I have been in my younger years, but it has taken me a lifetime trying to catch up and a lot of excessive drinking and drug abuse along the way. This drinking and using only helped to keep me emotionally undeveloped and immature. I am becoming more aware of many of these issues, but it has been a lifetime struggle toward self-awareness and consciousness.

**

For Adele, it was opiates. How closely should we link contact with her authoritarian stepfather and a heroin addiction? Here is her story:

**

The authoritarian in my life, from when I was 11 until I was 28 years old, was my stepfather. He was a former Marine and a preacher and had been raised by a mother who had been married to two alcoholic men (his father and his stepfather). As for me, I walked on eggshells constantly. I felt inhibited and suppressed; I became hypervigilant regarding loud noises because he had a tendency to "snap." My mother and sister are very passive people and would not stand up to him.

I would get into severe arguments and yelling matches with him whenever I felt that I could not suppress my angry feelings any more – I have an impulsivity behavior disorder (ADHD, combined type). I became a very rebellious person and had a tendency to "strike first" to keep people from hurting me. It has taken me years to smooth away the rough edges I accrued in that family. I'm told that I still exhibit a "chip-on-the-shoulder" attitude when I'm not attending to my state of mind.

Every time I stood up to him, my mother and sister would get angry at me because I was "making things worse." This caused a lot of strain in my relationship with both of them. I remember being at a family function at the age of 25 and I disagreed with him on some minor point. I had explained that the person's behavior was most likely due to the culture he was raised in. The next day when I stopped in to see my mother, he said to me, "Never disagree with me in front of family again." This was my mother's side of the family, they are very open to argument, and I was an adult!

I think he liked to think of himself as a leader, as he had narcissistic personality traits. I feel like whenever he would act humble or passive that it was a show – he liked to present himself as the epitome of Christian masculinity. That would probably make him a leader since he was so well respected among the church community. He definitely is an authoritarian personality – he didn't have much of a parenting style. The house rules were pretty much, "My way or the highway."

As to the consequences on me, I tend to feel like people are out to get me. It's not so much of a paranoia issue but as a defensive response from always having to be on guard. That is another consequence – I am a very guarded person and it takes a long time for me to warm up to people. I feel that if I allow myself to care about someone that they will have the ability to control me.

On the exterior, I am a very controlled person. Those that know me well are very accustomed to "emergency" calls, in which I am incredibly angry or anxious.

As mentioned before, I have ADHD and I also have a history of drug addiction (eight years clean – opiates). I have since stopped blaming him for my use but I would be fooling myself if I didn't consider it a factor. I am still an escapist at heart, as well. While I may not use damaging items like heroin anymore, I like videogames, books, hiking, and binging on television shows. At work, I developed a plan with my supervisor for when I become overwhelmed, and it's called "Escape Plan." I "run away" for a short break and take a drive around campus.

I have been in three significant relationships (two years, five years, and seven years) that I have ended because my partner pushed me for marriage, despite me declaring early in each relationship that I never wanted to be married (control issues again). I will say that I communicate well with people and clients who have difficult personalities. I read body language really well, have a scary (physical) reaction time, and always have a contingency plan. I am considered a very patient person. However, I can become aggressive instead of assertive when I am not staying conscious of my state of mind. So, while I feel there were many negative consequences, including issues of addiction and escapism, it has been a mixed bag.

As to my healing, I addressed a lot of resentments through 12-step recovery (Narcotics Anonymous). I also went into treatment in 2009 – a six-month program. I went through CBT, DBT, and individual counseling with a psychologist. CBT worked wonders for me and it was partially because it provided a little bit of control over my life again. I discussed a lot of my rebellious behavior, escapism, and spiritual issues with my psychologist. I learned the difference between "aggressive" and "assertive" and worked on my self-esteem a lot. Therapy was invaluable to me and I still utilize the skills I was taught.

My profession also helps me keep these ideas fresh in my head (I am an LSW pursuing LISW). I keep trusted confidantes, mentors, and friends close to me. I don't keep many people in my social circle, but the ones I do know the right thing to say to me when I need it. One of the biggest factors in the healing process is realizing that it is a process and I need to forgive myself when I'm not perfect. I try to give myself affirmations when I act out in a positive manner rather than acting out of fear or anger. I'm known for being a bit antiauthoritarian at work and I enjoy challenging people and questioning the status quo. I'm accepted for that among my peers and feel that I am valued for it, as well.

As to any mental disorder diagnoses, the diagnosis "ADHD, combined type" was given to me as a diagnosis when I was six years old, before my stepfather was involved. He did not believe in mental health disorders and when he married my mother – I no longer received treatment for it. Now I am treated for ADHD but have since received a diagnosis of generalized anxiety, and I have a history of major depression (e.g., suicide attempt in 2009). I haven't received a diagnosis of excoriation, but my cuticles scream it loud and clear. I sometimes have a hard time determining whether some of my symptoms, like the hypervigilance, are from living in that household or are from having ADHD and a history of opiate addiction. I certainly wouldn't doubt that the anxiety stems from living in that household.

Luckily, my mother divorced him a couple years ago. I get along better with my mother and my sister now, and I don't dread visiting them. Prior to that, I did not speak with him except when I had to at family functions and at my mother's home. When I left treatment, I decided to cut him out of my life because I felt he was a negative influence. I have no guilt for the things I have said to him in the past, and I don't miss him. I feel (and felt) much saner, and I enjoy not having the chaos he always brought into our lives. As bad as it sounds, I heard what he's doing with his life, and I felt a delicious sense of pleasure because of all his current troubles.

What have I learned? I don't allow people to walk over me. I employ direct eye contact and square my body up when needed. I feel that how I present myself keeps me from being a target with an authoritarian. It's interesting, though, that I can usually spot an authoritarian, but I'm not sure what I notice in them that triggers that recognition.

To anyone, I would recommend therapy. Be honest and open with a therapist. Practice self-affirmations and being assertive. Tell yourself that you have just as much say as anyone else and just as many rights. Practice accepting imperfection in yourself and others. Exercise your vulnerability – everyone doesn't have an authoritarian personality and **SOME** people really aren't out to control you or hurt you!

* *

19

CONSEQUENCES: PHYSICAL COMPLAINTS

We live in an age of physical complaints whose exact biological, organic, or "disease" causes are often hard to pin down. To say that many of them may have to do with prior or current trauma isn't to say that they are psychosomatic or psychological in nature. Rather, that's to say that trauma, stress, and psychological wounding naturally, logically – and often severely – play themselves out in the body.

No one doubts that there is a mind/body connection. People find it a little harder to accept that past unresolved traumas and ongoing present traumas can produce illness. We hate to think that we've opened ourselves up to respiratory problems, digestive problems, other physical ailments and medical conditions, and even chronically poor health because of the way our mind works and the way our personality has formed as a result of trauma. But that's exactly what a mind/body connection implies. Our mental, emotional, and psychological states affect our physical health.

The British National Health Service puts it this way:

> Trauma is a term used to describe single or multiple distressing events that may have long lasting and harmful effects on a person's physical and/or emotional well-being. There is a direct correlation between trauma and physical health conditions such as diabetes, COPD, heart disease, cancer, and high blood pressure.

The physical ailments and illnesses that result from unresolved trauma are anything but psychosomatic. Trauma-informed physical care connects the dots between unresolved trauma and physical illness rather than belittling or discounting an ailment as "merely" psychosomatic. If, for example, my hair turns white overnight because my child has been kidnapped, that is a stress-induced physical reaction to a traumatic event and not a self-induced psychosomatic reaction. I didn't make my hair turn white by "not being strong enough" to deal with this event in a stress-free way or by "not getting over" the kidnapping as if nothing in particular had happened.

Likewise, if you've been traumatized by an authoritarian you ought not to blame yourself for a physical ailment precipitated by the wounding, you ought not to feel embarrassed or humiliated because you "let yourself" get sick by not being "mentally strong enough" to avoid illness, and you ought not to allow others to shame you, blame you, or discount the way that the traumatizing person acted as an agent in your illness or ailment.

It can prove hard not to feel embarrassed or ashamed, especially if you've continued your own wounding by entering into serial relationships with authoritarians. You may feel that, for those repeated mistakes at least, there really is no one else to blame but yourself, and that therefore you really did cause your own ailments. Looking at the matter that way sounds plausible but it actually discounts the power of trauma to "keep on giving." Human beings are just not built that well to get over trauma easily, which is why early trauma and adverse childhood experiences matter so much.

Unfortunately, what this also means is that, like the authoritarian who harmed you and who exhibited moral bankruptcy by inflicting that harm, you may have taken the ethical low ground yourself by, for instance, siding with an authoritarian and not caring for those in your charge, by over-punishing and under-loving, by creating or aligning with arbitrary or sadistic rules, and so on. Blame and guilt are not the issues now: doing the right thing from here on out is. One of those "right things" is to recognize the powerful connection between authoritarian wounding and physical illness and to do what's required to heal both the emotional and physical.

Let's look at one story. Only after many years of repeating unfortunate relationship patterns and dealing with physical ailments did Anna come to recognize the connection between her authoritarian father's wounding behaviors and her own lifelong difficulties. Her journey is not over, and her healing is not complete, but the awareness she can now bring to her patterns and the connections she can now make between traumatic wounding and illness are important steps forward.

Anna explained:

My father was the authoritarian in my life. Living with him was disturbing and humiliating. He was completely unpredictable and alternated between being loving and kind and irrational authoritarian aggressiveness. He was a police officer and an Army reservist and at times he would treat me as if he were interrogating a suspect or as if I were a raw recruit in basic training. He was constantly on the lookout for "offenses" that I might have committed. All went reasonably well – as long as I did things exactly his way.

I would say that he was authoritarian through and through, although he could be empathic and charming in order to get his way. As a result of the way he treated me, I have always had great difficulty in making choices that are "selfish" or that are the best for me. Instead I compromise and try to make the other person happy and then I resent the situation. I struggle to admit that I have made these subjugating choices and I still find it hard to take the action to break away.

I have married partners, not once but three times, that are controlling, and I have lived in a subjugated and self-sacrificing way. Each time I married I had to leave my town and my friends and community to move to my partner's town, where I would then have to restart my life and my career. It's a clear life pattern that I have come to acknowledge only this year.

A major consequence of maintaining this position of subjugation has been recurring migraine headaches and asthma throughout my life. These illnesses flare up when I am very tense, when I continue to suppress my unmet needs, and when I well up with resentment. I have struggled to recognize this reality for most of my life. However, it has finally become clear to me that, wounded the way I was, I became a self-subjugating and self-sacrificing person who has difficulties being assertive when it comes to expressing my needs, beliefs, goals, and heart-felt desires, and all this suppression makes me physically ill.

The physical ailments we're talking about can take many forms. One class of ailments that is epidemic is the class of sleep disorders. How many of the 80,000,000 Americans reporting sleep disorders have had their sleeplessness caused by authoritarian contact? It could be a great many. Here is Melanie's story:

> The authoritarian in my life was my ex-husband. The experience was traumatizing. I was already prone to anxiety, which worsened, and I started to have physical side effects from stressors and lack of sleep. Every decision I made in my life was filtered through what he would want or how he would respond to my decisions.
>
> Based on my relationship with him, I had contemplated death by suicide because I damaged so many relationships and believed everyone would be better off without me. He (and I) had me convinced that I was worthless. Toward the end of the relationship, I developed a circadian rhythm disorder due to only getting three to four hours of sleep a night. I also dealt with years of trauma-related symptoms: hypervigilance, nightmares, an exaggerated startle response, anxiety, and flashbacks. When I finally forgave my ex-husband (unbeknownst to him) in March of 2016 (we had been separated since October 2009), my nightmares instantly stopped. It was incredible.
>
> I had already been struggling with anxiety for years prior although it progressively worsened. I had already demonstrated mild anxiety (which I did not recognize), then

started dating him when I was 17, around the same time my parents separated. I clung to him through their divorce, going to college, the losses of my grandparents, and my mom's cancer diagnosis and eventual passing. He was the only constant and I didn't recognize his abusive and controlling traits until it was too late.

When I broke up with him, I felt guilty initially. The night we finally separated he threatened to kill himself and made other threats, too. I felt very responsible. Every time he called I thought I had to answer the phone. I was terrified to let it go to voicemail. When he stalked me in public, I thought I had to be nice and have a polite conversation with him. As more time passed and I gained more confidence and safety, I gradually felt saner.

I was very fearful for a long time. What has helped? Supportive friends and family. Learning how to open up to people and not hide my wounds. Improving my personal boundaries with others. I've found people I trust, people I can talk to, people who value me, who love me, and who listen. And I am sleeping so much better!

We also mustn't forget the literal physical consequences of authoritarian aggression: the physical consequences of beatings and burnings, of malnutrition or an absence of dental care, etc. A victim's scars may well be physical as well as emotional. Here respondent Bob was left with a shortened leg for life. Bob explained:

Both my father and my stepfather were authoritarians. My mother was attracted to them because of her background. After my father cracked her head open, which I witnessed, she left him and released him from any responsibility. I learned from this that my family was terrifying and that I wanted to escape. I also learned that my father didn't value me enough to fight for custody and I felt the abandonment strongly, which I was forbidden to discuss. This all happened before I was one and I have memories from this early time because of the trauma.

I learned that if my mother was upset enough, you could be banished, and so I spent my childhood apologizing. I remember one instance when all of the children in our group thought to improve the look of the field next to our homes by painting the abandoned kitchen cabinets that had sat out for a very long time. At seven I was the oldest. The "paint" we used we found in the garage and was a mixture of old paint and turpentine. When we proudly revealed our gift, there was tremendous fury. My stepfather targeted me as the oldest, stripped me in front of everyone, and beat me. I carried bruises for over a week.

When I broke my ankle at the age of thirteen, I was humiliated into "walking it off" for a day instead of being taken to the emergency room. My leg is short now because of this. Another time, I was pushed back into the corner of a bar because of something I said to my stepfather, injuring my tailbone. That there was a sexual component to this was obvious to me. My stepfather was a leader, gregarious and always appreciated by his colleagues. He was charming, loud, opinionated ... and a racist and an authoritarian.

Among the negative consequences have been self-doubt, guilt, shame, and hypervigilance. Also, a craving for attention and approval, since these were often withheld. And, of course, that shorter leg. But I am healing. What's helped? Feeling my feelings. Positive self-talk and self-love. Recovery from addiction. Choosing not to respond to control and violence with violence. And CBT training for depression. That has helped me to focus on the future and to make letting go of the past a priority.

I am still in contact with my mother. This Christmas I called, but neither my brother nor stepfather requested to speak to me or I to them. I have no idea how to heal this or if it is even worth the effort. I feel furious at being made to feel the scapegoat and less than a stepchild even, and I no longer feel called to beg for attention and for their favor. However, there is another part of me that longs for peace and harmony in our relationship. All I can do is heal my thoughts and try to attract better people into my life. It's hard to be guilty or ashamed or manipulated when you are legitimately doing your best. That's what I'm trying to do.

In my experience, most of my clients are dealing with one major physical complaint or another. Of course, most of these are not connected to authoritarian wounding. But some are – and many more than we might suppose. Trauma and stress produce physical consequences, many of which are clusters of ailments with no accurate name.

Often clients spend their whole adult lives with mysterious, disabling physical complaints that no pills or treatments seem able to cure. In some of these cases, it may be that the wounded victim needs non-medical healing that takes into account the trauma that he or she experienced and that focuses on the emotional and the psychological as well as the physical.

We are bombarded by drug ads that make it seem as if every physical complaint must be medical or biological in nature and best (and maybe only) handled by a pill. However, if you believe in a mind/body connection and in the possibility that trauma and other profound events can cause or contribute to physical ailments, then you know better than to accept a too-easy drug solution. For any physical complaint that is undergirded by psychological causes, you won't find healing answers in a pill bottle.

20

CONSEQUENCES: REPETITION COMPULSION

Two headlines are that authoritarian wounds are long-lasting and that healing isn't easy. Making the process of healing much more difficult is that authoritarian wounding and personality formation are intertwined, causing, for example, repetitive behaviors that make no sense either to you or to your client.

Why is it that your client keeps involving herself with bullying men, even though she hated the experience of growing up with her bullying father? We can dream up explanations for this "repetition compulsion," calling it habit, masochism, or whatever we like, but we don't really understand these perplexing dynamics. And they make healing that much more complicated and iffy.

Many, perhaps even a majority, of the respondents to my Authoritarian Wound Questionnaire who experienced authoritarian wounding in childhood went on to pick an authoritarian mate. This "repetition compulsion" is hard to understand and the explanations that respondents tended to give, for instance, that they choose an authoritarian mate because it "felt familiar," don't feel like the whole story. Whatever the psychological reasons for this "repetition compulsion," it's important that as a helper you look for this possibility, expect this possibility, and have your ways of talking about it and dealing with it.

You will see in the following story, Roberta's story, one of the headlines of authoritarian wounding: a likelihood for the victim to choose a mate as authoritarian as the authoritarian parent with whom he or she grew up. As a helper, the following is important for you to remember: if your client reports an authoritarian parent, you will want to check in on whether there is now an authoritarian mate in the picture. Conversely, if your client reports an authoritarian mate, you will want to check in

CONSEQUENCES: REPETITION COMPULSION   145

on her childhood experiences and specifically inquire as to whether she grew up with an authoritarian parent or some other authoritarian family member such as a grandparent or sibling. Here is Roberta's story.

* *

I am now 65 years old and I have spent much of my life in recovery from my upbringing. My mother had an authoritarian personality, was probably clinically depressed, was maybe bipolar, and was certainly angry all the time. She could explode and strike out with verbal or physical abuse at the drop of a hat.

After her death, my father found many hidden bottles of wine around the house, so she was probably also an alcoholic. I was "chronologically" an only child, since my sisters were six years and eight years older than me. My father was in the army, and we traveled wherever he went, including Europe. He was mostly absent, somewhere "out on maneuvers," but I imagine he was absent so much so as to get away from my mother.

An incident that beautifully captures my experience occurred when I was about five years old and stung by a bee. I remember the searing pain, I remember crying and running to mother – only to be beaten for crying! I spent my childhood bending over backwards seeking her approval, but to no avail. My identity was founded on blending in with the woodwork so that I wouldn't be noticed and on never speaking up.

Homework was torture. I remember her drilling me on penmanship when I was in fourth or fifth grade, screaming at me and ripping one assignment up after another because I lifted the pencil off the paper between two connected letters. When I was 12 years old she decided that my waist-length hair was going to be cut short. Again, I had no say in the matter.

When my parents were together they fought constantly. It seems that nearly every family outing was marred by their fights. We went on a weekend trip to Paris and they had a fairly spectacular fight in the hotel room. As this was a tour made up of army personnel, at some point we had group photos taken, and I gravitated to the mother of a friend who was kind and loving, someone I stood next to in the photos. After we got the photos, my mother was furious that I hadn't stood next to her in Paris. I heard about that for many years.

I think my mother was more of an authoritarian follower than an authoritarian leader. She needed to impress others and her demand for perfection wasn't based on some principle but had more to do with what others thought of her: that is, that she was perceived as having perfect children, children who were seen but not heard and always on excellent behavior.

As mine was a military upbringing, my father would be notified of any problems that we had in school. It was my older sister, the middle daughter, who had the most troubles in school and who my father got the most complaints about. This didn't sit well with my mother, since according to the army "a soldier who can't control his children can't control a platoon" and so my sister's behavior reflected poorly on my father and the whole family. I believe my mother took those incidents with my sister personally and considered that she had shamed the family, which in turn provoked her rage against all of us.

I wouldn't say that my mother had an "authoritarian parenting style," as that implies some sort of choice in the matter. I think she was an authoritarian at her core. At that core, she lacked all control, which I think set her into a never-ending spin of hyper-controlling behavior. Much of my younger years I spent depressed and at times suicidal. I was a good student though, extremely creative, the student always pointed out as the "artist in the class."

When classmates said the things that they say about the class artist, things like "I hate you that you can do that so well" and "I hate people that can do that," my approval-seeking mind shut down my art. In high school, I began to experience panic to the point of being unable to function. I found it terribly hard to get through high school when you are expected to stand in front of the class and give reports; but I somehow managed to get through and go on to college.

I chose to go to college, though neither of my parents understood why. I attended a community college, majored in psychology, and lived at home. One incident stands out: I was 19 years old and my mother started beating me for not doing my laundry. I fought back this time, and then I ran away to my aunt's home and only returned several days later, not having told her where I was. She was furious; but after that she let me be.

I married the first man who came along. My choice was someone so much like my mother that it was unbelievable. He was eventually diagnosed bipolar and was also an alcoholic. I suspect I was drawn to the familiar. I went on to graduate school without any acknowledgement or recognition from my mother. My father supported my decision, but my mother thought I was trying to be better than her and let me know about her disapproval. I went on to receive a master's degree in occupational therapy from Columbia; my upbringing had drawn out of me a deep feeling of compassion for others who were traumatized, disenfranchised, imperfect, or disabled.

After my first child was born I lapsed into postpartum depression. When my son was three months old I found myself researching the cost of getting on a plane and traveling somewhere and never coming back. I was terrified of being a mother and being like my own mother. I was able to pull it together and find a therapist. She saved my life but she also set me on the course of either fixing my marriage or getting out of it. Getting out of it took me a long time, since shame and fear of failure were deeply ingrained in me, but we were eventually divorced after 32 years of marriage.

My sons were so precious to me. I tried so hard to be a good mother because I knew "what not to do" as a parent. Unfortunately, their father was an authoritarian. Sadly, my firstborn son committed suicide last year. He was 31 years old, he had been diagnosed with schizoaffective disorder, he was delusional and psychotic, and he refused to seek help. I suspect that his father's authoritarian nature and my lack of ability to set my own life straight could have been contributors to his death ... all because of the far-reaching effects of my authoritarian upbringing. In retrospect, I believe I did the best I could, given the circumstances.

After my mother died in 1990, I didn't cry at all. Instead I found an enormous sense of freedom and relief. I found the freedom to get a divorce, to sing, and to explore my suppressed artistic talents. Finding my voice through singing was a large component of my healing. I took voice lessons, joined singing groups, joined the Unitarian Church, and sang in the choir. I started attending singing workshops and even attended a three-week singing workshop in South Africa. There is nothing more healing than singing loud! Also, I recently completed yoga teacher training and exploring the chakras was fascinating. The throat chakra represents our personal power and freedom of expression. I believe that my throat chakra completely opened after my mother died.

In my earlier life, I had a great deal of difficulty with anyone who acted like my mother. Panic set in when I felt that nobody was listening to me, particularly when attending Columbia with a very authoritarian teacher. Certain aspects of therapy have helped, particularly my therapist pointing out the similarities in behavior between that teacher and my mother. This helped me in dealing with both of them. That helped, as did meds. I am a strong believer in meds allowing you to have success; then you can reduce the meds because you have learned how to handle the challenges better.

Counseling and meds helped with my inability to speak, much less sing, in front of a group of people. In the 1990s I was able to perform on stage for the first time in Christmas Revels because of Prozac. I went on to perform in other productions and found that after three years I could discontinue its use. I was also able to begin sharing my art, which was extremely difficult at first. But with therapy I got beyond that. I have had three therapists through the years; their guidance enabled me to go on to have a very rich and rewarding life in spite of so much pain. Yoga and learning to meditate have been extremely useful as well.

I have been diagnosed with major depression and anxiety disorder. I attribute both to my upbringing. Depression is not so much an issue as it used to be but anxiety can rear its ugly head. If, for instance, I wake up in the middle of the night, I can find all sorts of reasons to blame myself for my son's suicide. Reading the book *Motherless Daughters* was an eye-opener, as many of the symptoms experienced by daughters who lose their mothers were so similar to my own. Lacking a mother's love and lacking a mother's modeling how to be a woman and a mother leave you to your own devices to learn how to be in this world. Those women are lucky who have someone in life who can model becoming a woman and a mother.

My mother died when we were still in contact. Divorce from my authoritarian husband was traumatic. My husband stalked me and at times would verbally abuse me in public. It was frightening, but eventually he moved away, and yes, I did feel saner and safer once it was over. I knew I was doing the right thing. I am fortunate to no longer have an authoritarian in my life, unless you include our politicians. With regard to that, I make phone calls to senators and congressmen and try to stay active in resisting, and as a result I feel less powerless.

Here is the advice I would give someone dealing with an authoritarian:

- The fact that they are the way they are has nothing to do with you. Once I realized that, my life changed substantially. It is not your fault.
- Nurture yourself, provide yourself the nurturing you need, don't rely on others to do that.
- Give yourself permission to explore aspects of yourself that are unique to you.
- Find people who fill in the blanks, like mother or father substitutes, who hold up a mirror to your beauty and wisdom and, when you find them, spend time with them.
- Learn meditation and yoga, take walks in nature, sing, and express yourself in other ways. If you have trouble expressing yourself, start drawing or fiddling around with clay, or take up an instrument. If you can't afford lessons, there are plenty of instructional videos on YouTube.
- Stay present, in this moment. Yesterday and tomorrow don't exist really, do they? Staying in this moment will keep you from pondering the "what ifs" and "if onlys."

I still to this day mourn the loss of a nurturing mother and ponder what my life might have been like had my mother been different. Those thoughts no longer dominate my world like they once did, and in fact, the experience of growing up in an authoritarian environment actually contributed in making me more compassionate to the suffering of others and provided me with my life's work.

The pain we carry from a horrific upbringing can subside as we age, and we can become more like the person we were supposed to be if we take care of ourselves, find good therapists, find a supportive community, and find people who mirror our inherent goodness and give ourselves the permission to explore who we really are.

* *

21

WHAT YOU CAN EXPECT

Over the last several chapters, we've looked at some of the consequences of authoritarian wounding, among them depression, anxiety, addictions, physical complaints, and repetition compulsions. But there are additional consequences, and many of them are not so easy to name.

In this chapter, I want to let several respondents speak for themselves, so as to give you a fuller and rounder sense of how authoritarian wounding is experienced. This will help you better understand what issues may arise in session. What follows are brief excerpts from respondents' questionnaire responses.

Raymond explained:

> The authoritarian in my life was my stepfather. I was not allowed to express my opinion if my opinion contradicted his. I was not allowed to express anger. I was often not allowed to express disappointment. Rules and instructions were to be followed without question. Any of the above behaviors (expressing a different opinion from him, expressing anger or disappointment, and questioning rules and instructions) resulted in being yelled at, being told to "Watch your mouth" and "Don't give me no lip" and "Because I said so."
>
> I was usually intimidated enough that I acquiesced. On the rare occasion that I bucked, he became angry and threatening. I don't know if he would have done physical harm, but I was afraid that he would. The results? A fear of questioning authority. A fear of authority figures, especially males. A fear of punishment. Guilt. Difficulty being a Christian, because

I project my stepfather's authoritarianism on to Jesus. Difficulty and fear of expressing anger. And anxiety.

Audrey explained:

Here I am, a highly functioning person, yet I am crumbling and have even had some suicidal ideation, nothing serious, but I am struggling (and I am not even depressed, I don't think). It is really hard to describe. I was abused violently for the first 20 years of my life by my mother, and for the last 20 years, I've still had to be in a relationship with her, and I've developed very strong distortions in order to maintain this relationship.

Now in therapy, and finally not having a relationship with my mother, I am left to undo all these denials and projections and a seriously distorted self-identification (I identify completely with my mom). All the while I'm still working, in school and in a marriage. How can I do it? I have no self. I believe every single thing my mom thought of me for over 40 years. Of course, there is a part of me that is writing this and that is aware of that part of me that is healthy, but that part is very small and scared.

The part that split to become my mother is much more developed and powerful and if I undo it all, I am left with no self-agency at all. I know that this is the fear talking, the same part of me that wishes I was dead a long time ago and wished that I had never become my mother! But I am also hopeful. It is truly scary to be this damaged by a parent and then to stay with that parent and just destroy myself further just so as to have a mother! That is sick, sick, sick. But I am surviving ... but I am also tired of just surviving and I want to be healthy and have a normal life.

Lea explained:

My whole family was authoritarian and extremely negative. Those experiences caused me to feel a lot of negative emotions including anxiety, stress, and anger. The first thing that I can recall about my authoritarian family is how much they made me hate them. The personal consequences for me: number one is resistance to authority. An inability to accept the authority of my mother and a deep-rooted hatred for how my parents raised me. I always had a desire to leave home: freedom and privacy were everything.

At the same time, I was scared of losing control or being alone. Lots of sadness and anger. Hating life. I loved being a rebel or just acting out in unconventional ways and shocking everyone with controversial opinions. I've always hated being told I am not "normal" or that I'm "weird" or that something about me is "not good enough," because I know that everything is subjective and that terms like "normal" and "weird" are social constructs that are just used by those in power to keep people in line. They are there to ensure that they conform to certain standards. To repeat the headlines: I'm full of hate and I have this (not always very productive) need to rebel and act out.

Ingrid explained:

Both of my parents were authoritarians, especially my mother. The experience was horrible and emotionally wounding. It was mainly psychological abuse, which I am only now (at age 50) beginning to recognize and recover from. The consequences? Low self-esteem, lack of self-confidence, anxiety, depression, shyness, timidity, hesitation, extreme self-doubt, difficulties with decision-making, difficulties with bonding (no deep friendships), and difficulty trusting others due to never having received real and true parental love. And the following as well: a sense of guilt, feeling guilty and responsible for absolutely everything, like I'm at fault and faulty. And an all-pervasive sense of dread (I often feel like something really bad is about to happen and when it does, it will all be my fault).

Denise explained:

> I grew up with a damaged sense of self, knowing intellectually that I had positive traits, yet always feeling anxious and shy when I had to perform. I also was depressed because I grew up being invalidated, and without a feeling of love or support. My mother used to say things like "What do you want, love and understanding?" with heavy sarcasm. My relationships, both friendly and romantic, have been "off" in many ways. I also emerged out of adolescence into adulthood without a sense of direction. I really had no idea what to do. And when I finally did make some choices and acted on them, it was almost always with a lack of confidence, and feeling like a fraud.

Denise explained:

> The consequences were both good and bad. I am compassionate and I listen. I am independent, educated, and strong. I do not hit anything or anyone. I am extremely attached and good with animals. I used to "spank" my pets (lightly). Then one day, I looked at the fear in my cat's eyes, and I was done with that. I realized those eyes were my eyes. I yell, not often, but I do.
>
> However, I am terrified when my spouse yells, which is not often. I have trust issues (more to do with my sister than my father. My sister (we're both adopted) is sociopathic. I had a penchant, more than 35 years ago, to become involved with very protective men. That led to various levels of abuse. That's over and done with: I've been with my current kind husband for 38 years. I'm intuitive but I am also oversensitive at times. As I say, the good and the bad together.

Authoritarian wounding will produce a variety of negative consequences and completely idiosyncratic packages of consequences. Your clients are real human beings who have built a complex personality, partly but not wholly in response to authoritarian contact. What can you expect to see? Plenty of complexity! Lee Jampolsky, author of *Healing the Addictive Personality* and developer of inspirational psychology, provided me with the following schema of what in his opinion you can expect to see. Lee explained:

> As I see it, there are four primary authoritarian behaviors which each lead to certain consequences.
>
> Behavior 1: Tells, preaches, coerces, demands, shames, and enforces. Dialogue and other opinions discouraged.
>
> Result: Fear-based environment and internalized anger results in either a shrinking of self or unconsciously mimicking the authoritarian behavior.
>
> Behavior 2: No feedback or input sought or desired, and if expressed, met with ridicule, attack, deflection, and punishment.
>
> Result: Lack of strong sense of Self and delayed or repressed intellectual/cognitive development, or unconsciously mimicking the authoritarian behavior.
>
> Behavior 3: All goals, tasks, and decisions created by "leader," but no or low responsibility taken on any negative outcomes.
>
> Result: Development of conflicting or absent goals and lack of life direction, or unconsciously mimicking the authoritarian behavior.
>
> Behavior 4: Lack of demonstrated trust and value in others while demanding trust and loyalty.
>
> Result: Lack of trust in self and others, or unconsciously mimicking the authoritarian behavior.

A central question that helpers must address is how to help a person in distress whose distress is so-to-speak built into his or her system and is an ingrained feature of personality. We are not seeing "symptoms" of something but rather the consequences of the complex interaction of original personality (who the person was at birth, with his or her own blueprint, endowments, and proclivities), formed personality (the particular accretion of personality over time in response to experiences and developed in self-conversation), and available personality (the individual's remaining freedom to make real change and to be who he or she decides to be).

Therefore, what can you expect? A real person. Someone who in one session wants to feel better and who in another session has rather given up again, who in one session feels some hope and who in another session is in despair again, who in one session announces a very keen insight and who in the next session announces that he or she has engaged in all the behaviors he or she pledged to no longer countenance. Anyone who has tried to help real human beings knows how unpredictable these encounters can be, where with one client something important transpires in ten minutes and the road to significant change is embraced, with another client all that seems to go on is a kind of stasis punctuated by insights, pledges, and no actual change, and with a third client a worsening occurs, because the client quickly realizes that you, like other helpers, can't help him or her enough.

You can also expect that you may find yourself focusing on some particular "small" thing that is actually not small at all because it both represents an opening for healing and a kind of recapitulation of everything that your client has experienced and is trying to remedy. For example, I was working with a world-famous painter who was dreading a series of studio visits from collectors and museum representatives. She was so well known that for each of these two visits, the one from collectors and the one from museum representatives, her "guests" would be arriving by chartered bus, so many of them were there and so keen was the interest in her latest work.

If you didn't understand human beings, you might exclaim, "How wonderful for her!" She, however, was dreading the visits. She had grown up with two authoritarian parents who shamed her, punished her for being herself, and made her feel small and worthless. She had fought back from this harm through a great deal of personal work, which included mindfulness meditation, yoga, therapy, coaching, self-help books, and more. She had gotten to the point in her life where in the studio she felt powerful; in the studio, she felt healed. But when exposing new work to strangers, whom she characterized as vultures, she got small again and would often either get sick and cancel the studio visit or act out and make scenes.

So, while we spent several sessions on what might be thought of as the "small matter" of two upcoming studio visits, we were in fact doing real and important work in the areas of authoritarian wounding and authoritarian healing. What should be underlined is that we had named authoritarian wounding as an issue and knew that, in addition to whatever else we were working on, we were also (and in a sense always) working on healing that wound. That is, we had gotten authoritarian wounding named as both an issue and as an important issue. Many questionnaire respondents reported that their authoritarian wounding never did get named in the course of their therapy and so remained unaddressed. Let's look at that next: how you can get that issue on the table in session.

22

BRINGING UP AUTHORITARIAN WOUNDING

In my experience, clients are absolutely clear about whether or not one of their parents, or someone else close to them, was or is an authoritarian. But almost to a one, they have not been asked that question directly in therapy, counseling, or coaching. It is one of those adverse childhood experiences or adverse adult experiences that doesn't get named. Furthermore, in the current model of diagnosing mental disorders, where causes are not considered relevant, information of that sort has no particular place.

As a result, more often than not a client's authoritarian wounding isn't brought up and doesn't get addressed. It is therefore on the shoulders of helpers to ask that question and to get that matter on the table. Imagine that something affecting perhaps the majority of your clients and directly related to your client's depression, anxiety, or addiction never got addressed? Wouldn't you want to remedy that situation? But how? How exactly might helpers elicit information from their clients about their authoritarian wounds?

As it currently stands, with helpers unaccustomed to checking in about authoritarian wounding, you might work with a client for years and never hear about a bullying sibling or a cruel grandparent. Yet your client's childhood experiences with that authoritarian were not only damaging and likely to have risen to the level of trauma, but they have contributed to her formed personality, to the way in which she is overly-anxious or despairing today. Likewise, as an adverse childhood or adult experience that created or is still creating toxic stress, it likely is affecting her current physical health as well as her emotional well-being.

Without your help, she may never make the connection between being beaten by her grandmother and her early school failures or the connection between being beaten by her grandmother and her *current* problems with work, with her own children, with her mate, or with her self-confidence and self-image. Nor is she likely to make connections between those experiences and her problems with her immune system, her sleep habits, or her energy levels. You can help her make those connections and then help her make the difficult changes that are essential parts of the healing process – but only if the matter comes up.

How will you bring it up? How you bring the matter up is a function of how you work. Say, for example, that you are a coach who doesn't take history – who instead works in the here and now to help clients set goals and who then monitors your clients' progress toward achieving those goals. Working this way, you're unlikely to introduce any historical questioning at all – maybe not until a client consistently fails to meet her goals and a conversation about the past becomes mandatory. Only then might you tentatively – and perhaps quite reluctantly – ask about your client's past.

At that point, you might inquire for the first time about authoritarian wounding as one of the several historical questions that you ask. If, as a coach, you have gotten into the habit of not asking about *anything* historical, this would amount to quite a stretch and quite a change in the way you work. Indeed, now might prove a good time to think through whether you want to find some careful ways of introducing historical investigating into your method of working. Is it possible that at a certain point you would supply your client with a formal questionnaire or with an informal set of questions? Or you might simply ask your client, "What in your past do you think might be contributing to your present challenges?"

The above question doesn't get at authoritarian wounding per se and therefore is a fine question to ask as a first question but probably not the only question you would want to ask. You might at some point follow up your initial historical investigations with the wonder, "You know, I never asked you directly about whether you grew up with an authoritarian, maybe a parent or a sibling or someone else? Did you have that experience? Or might there currently be an authoritarian in your life?" As I've mentioned, clients have no trouble understanding what you mean by an authoritarian and don't need you to define "authoritarian" or add anything else by way of clarification. They will understand your question and, if they are ready to answer, feel safe enough to answer, and aren't triggered by the question, will want to answer.

Of course, they may initially not feel safe enough. You likely will have to gain their trust over time. Remember how important client safety and client readiness are in working with traumatized clients. In whatever ways that you ask your questions and however you investigate past traumas, you will want to tread lightly, go slowly, and know how to back off without giving up on the investigation.

Remember that you aren't conducting an interrogation or rushing down some checklist, as you might if you were hunting for symptoms or symptom pictures. Rather, you are honoring the difficulty that your client may be experiencing acknowledging this wounding, thinking about this wounding, and discussing this wounding – especially considering how ashamed the subject may make him or her feel.

In my current primary work as a creativity coach, now that I've retired as a family therapist, I do not ask for historical information as a client and I begin our work together and I don't tend to elicit historical information as we work in an ongoing way together. This is because coaching is very present-oriented, future-oriented, and goal-oriented. But I do ask the following three questions of all new clients:

1 *Can you start by describing your situation a little? What sort of art do you do, what's been your history with art-making and art-selling, what ups and downs have you experienced, and so*

on? Please write as little or as much as you like — but enough to give me a starting picture of "where you're at and where you've been."

2   What are your biggest challenges right now, either internal or external, with respect to your creative life?

3   What would you like to accomplish over the next few months with respect to your creative life? Do you maybe have some "minimum goals" and also some "Wow, that would be great!" goals?

These simple, nonintrusive questions, which do not "pull" for any clinical information or family-of-origin information, nevertheless get me a lot of information about my client's creative life but also about his or her family-of-origin and his current family circumstances. These "innocent" questions seem to get under a client's radar and allow him or her to share important, difficult information with me. As a rule, a new client will write a lengthy response that is frank about everything from past abuse to current despair.

Along the same lines, and taking the tack that "simple" might prove very effective, what if you asked new clients just the following three questions: (1) Can you tell me a little bit about your childhood? (2) Does anything about your childhood seem particularly difficult or troubling? (3) Does anything in your current situation seem to connect back to your childhood? Don't you have the suspicion that those three "innocent" questions would get you a wealth of material, including direct information or indirect clues about any authoritarian wounding?

What if you are a mental health nurse or other helper in a certain sort of constrained setting where "helping" primarily means monitoring the psychiatric meds that patients are taking or monitoring the behavioral goals that the institution sets for patients? Then you may find yourself with no easy way to ask such questions, no easy way to elicit much information, and maybe no real permission to do any investigating. In that case, you may find that dropping your wonders about authoritarian wounding (and the other wonders you may have about your patients' historical challenges) into the casual conversations that you have with patients, conversations that are likely among their most healing interactions, is the very best way and perhaps the only way to operate.

When your institution or your situation doesn't allow for much checking in about your client's reality, you may have to accomplish that checking in off the cuff and between the lines. This is hardly ideal; a quick conversation, loose boundaries, or an off-the-cuff remark can trigger a traumatized person and not prove helpful. The flip side is that if the traumatized person never has a chance to talk about what is real for him or her, it may be worth the risk to engage informally if that is all that your setting and circumstances allow.

If you're a psychiatrist, the extent to which you bring these matters up will of course largely depend on whether or not you engage in psychotherapy with your patients or whether you rely entirely on the pseudo-medical model of diagnosing your patients and then providing them with chemicals that you then monitor. In that scenario, monitoring those chemicals becomes your primary ongoing work with patients. If you are a psychiatrist of this sort, then historical material doesn't concern you and you will remain studiously incurious about your patient's authoritarian wounding or anything else that may have happened to her. If, however, you are a psychiatrist who also functions as a psychotherapist or counselor and who takes an interest in your patient's history, then you would want to learn about her wounding in whatever ways that you learn about historical information.

And what if you work in a nondirective way with clients and rarely lead them? It is then remarkably easy for the trauma of authoritarian wounding never to come up in therapy, in part because of the way you work, relying on your client to lead the therapy, and in part because authoritarian wounding is likely not on your "mental checklist" of adverse childhood experiences. Remember that clients are not inclined to bring up shameful material in session (or anywhere) and that they may be very practiced at telling "the same old story" (and coming to the same conclusions) as a way to avoid pain. For these reasons and for other reasons as well, even a therapist interested in eliciting historical information may not hear about her client's authoritarian wounding – and may therefore miss the chance to be of that much more help.

This circles us back to a fundamental question: how does *any* helper learn about her client's historical reality? Virtually all models of psychotherapy, whether they are based on a symptom-hunt, diagnose-and-treat model, on a traditional theoretical orientation (like Freudian psychoanalysis), on a seat-of-your-pants, "let's chat about whatever you bring up" way of working, on a system or style (like cognitive-behavioral therapy), or something else, do not have built into them any formal or systematic way of learning about what happened to clients. Indeed, virtually all private-practice mental health practitioners rather scorn history taking and avoid systematic history taking.

In part, this avoidance and reluctance make sense. Would clients be capable of filling out elaborate, lengthy historical questionnaires? Would they be willing to fill them out? Would they feel comfortable engaging in all that revealing with a stranger? Would they feel safe? Would helpers want to read all that "for free" and take the time to make sense of their clients' history? Would clients appreciate spending large portions of sessions answering questions about the past? Would they find such divulging relevant, especially if they've bought into the dominant model and are hoping for a diagnosis and a chemical fix? Would they accept being steered in such ways if they came in complaining about marital problems or depression? In short, would clients prove willing and helpful or unwilling and resentful?

Both realities seem to me to be true, that it is relevant and maybe even vital to know about the extent to which your client has been wounded by her contact with an authoritarian *and* that it isn't a straightforward matter to acquire such information (or any other relevant historical information). You could of course thoroughly remake your helping style so as to learn more about your clients and their historical circumstances. That would amount to a big makeover for most helpers and might also likely fly in the face of a given helper's basic stance (say, for instance, as nondirective), her theoretical orientation, her ability to accept insurance payments, or the requirements of her institution.

Likewise, it might fly in the face of her sense of how best to spend what may be a very limited amount of time with clients and even her sense of what actually helps (feeling, for instance, that dealing with negative self-talk is more important than historical excavating). Any helper curious about increasing his or her focus on historical material and engaging in a big makeover would have to take all of this into account.

A helper might do the following simpler thing instead. You might do a little rethinking about how best to learn some important headlines about your client's historical reality. Your internal guiding question might be, *Knowing something about my client's history must be useful. How can I learn that "little something" in such a way that my investigating is only minimally intrusive and that it doesn't contradict or interfere with my basic way of working?*

How might you "simply" learn about the harm done to your clients as a result of authoritarian wounding? Give that question the thought it deserves. While you ponder that, let's move on to the next important matter: how you can more effectively help your traumatized clients. Let's examine that over the next several chapters.

23

TRAUMA-INFORMED CARE

We have been aware of the extent to which trauma causes harm for a very long time. But, as a rule, that truth has been more rejected than accepted by helpers and by the mental health establishment. Why this is the case is easy to understand. As a class, the same individuals who do the traumatizing are also in charge of deciding a society's paradigms. The government that sends you to war does not also want to admit that war is traumatizing. The religion that is highly dogmatic and punitive does not also want to admit that dogma and punishment traumatize. The corporation that acts in an authoritarian way toward its employees does not want to admit that they are harming their employees psychologically. And a mental health profession that relies on governments, corporations, religions, and other institutions for its prestige and very survival is likely to downplay – or even completely deny – the role of trauma in emotional life.

Jonathan Tomlinson explained, on his blog, "A Better National Health Service,"

> In 1896, Freud presented the detailed case histories of 18 women with "hysteria" – what might these days be labelled "Emotionally Unstable Personality disorder." In every case the women described childhood sexual abuse. Freud thought that he had found the source of hysteria and presented his findings in anticipation of fame and possibly fortune. What he failed to anticipate was that the upper echelons of Viennese society were not prepared to accept that

women with hysteria could be telling the truth and in so doing, implicating their own, privileged social circles. Freud was sent away to come up with another, more acceptable theory. His insights were buried and forgotten for most of the 20th century.

This rejection of the profound, sometimes causal relationship between trauma and emotional difficulties essentially continues to this day. In a mental health industry dominated by the pseudo-medical mental disorder paradigm and its chemical fix solutions, the idea that certain experiences, and not broken plumbing or other biological shortfalls, may be causing the things called depression, anxiety, addiction, etc., is still roundly dismissed. Life histories are not seen as particularly relevant, or even as slightly irrelevant, to the task of diagnosing and treating so-called mental disorders. Not only does this profitable, self-serving prejudice continue to this day, but it is also spreading, as its purveyors cast their nets ever wider in their efforts to sell pills to the whole world.

At the same time, largely connected to the aftermath of the Vietnam War and the explosion of PTSD survivors, a growing segment of the helping professions, especially in the nursing and social work spheres, began to take trauma seriously. The phrase "trauma-informed care" gained cachet and ideas as to what trauma-informed care might look like began to gain a foothold. As Chase Wilson, Donna Pence, and Lisa Conradi explain in "Trauma-Informed Care" in *The Encyclopedia of Social Work*:

> Following the Vietnam War, professional understanding of post-traumatic stress disorder (PTSD) increased. The greater understanding of trauma and its effects on war veterans has extended to informing our comprehension of trauma in the civilian world and with children and families who have experienced abuse, neglect, and other traumatic events. The concepts of trauma-informed care have evolved over the past 30 years from a variety of streams of thought and innovation. They are now being applied in a wide range

of settings, from mental health and substance-abuse treatment providers to child welfare systems and even schools and criminal justice institutions. In the simplest terms, the concept of trauma-informed care is straightforward.

If professionals were to pause and consider the role trauma and lingering traumatic stress plays in the lives of the specific client population served by an individual, professional, organization, or an entire system, how would they behave differently? What steps would they take to avoid, or at least minimize, adding new stress or inadvertently reminding their clients of their past traumas? How can they better help their traumatized clients heal? In effect, by looking at how the entire system is organized and services are delivered through a "trauma lens," what should be done differently? The answer can be used to guide practice, policy, procedures, and even how the physical caregiving environment is structured.

What are some of the approaches, principles, and practices of trauma-informed care? As with any large idea that allows for countless subjective interpretations, there is no single "trauma-informed care." But the following vision will serve us as we examine this idea. Myrna Schnur explained on the Lippincott Nursing Center blog:

There are four essential approaches and six principles of trauma-informed care.

The four essential approaches of trauma-informed care can be found in a program, organization, or system that:

1 *Realizes the widespread impact of trauma and understands potential paths for recovery.*
2 *Recognizes the signs and symptoms of trauma in clients, families, staff, and others.*
3 *Responds by fully integrating knowledge about trauma into policies, procedures, and practices.*
4 *Seeks to actively resist re-traumatization.*

The six key principles of trauma-informed care include:

1 Safety – make sure your patient and family members feel safe, both physically and psychologically.
2 Trustworthiness and transparency – trust between patients, staff, and management is vital in building strong relationships.
3 Peer support – identifying individuals with similar experiences of trauma helps to create safety, builds trust, enhances collaboration, and promotes recovery and healing.
4 Collaboration and mutuality – emphasize that all members of the team, including patients, are equal.
5 Empowerment, voice, and choice – identify individual strengths and differences and utilize them as the foundation for recovery and healing. Provide the patient with choices and an opportunity to share in the decision-making process, which results in a sense of control.
6 Recognition of cultural, historical, and gender issues – set aside cultural stereotypes and biases.

How does trauma-informed care look in session? Barbara Markway, on her "Living the Questions" blog for *Psychology Today*, provided the following example:

> Caitlyn had been to several mental health professionals for ongoing depression, but hadn't gotten better. She felt that none of the therapists understood her. In addition to her mood symptoms, Caitlyn experienced periods of time where she felt very out of control, sometimes cutting her arms with a razor blade. She did not want to die, but some of her past therapists had hospitalized her every time she talked about her cutting.
>
> Caitlyn was about ready to give up all hope of counseling helping her when she had a different experience with a new therapist. Caitlyn hesitated in mentioning her 'self-mutilation,' as her other therapists called it, but when she finally did, this therapist responded differently than the others. The previous therapists had asked questions suggesting there was something wrong with her, but this one gently said, "I wonder if something traumatic has happened to you. Would you like to talk about it?"

In that transformative moment, Caitlyn felt safe enough to begin discussing her traumatic childhood experiences. Through her tone and her words, the therapist communicated that there was nothing wrong with her, and that her cutting behavior was a way she had learned to cope with a horrific experience. What made the difference? Her therapist had been trained in Trauma-Informed Care (TIC).

If you'd like to operate in a trauma-informed-care way with your clients who have been wounded and traumatized by authoritarian contact, here are five practices you might adopt.

Be Mindful of Client Safety Issues

All clients need to feel safe but trauma victims have an even greater need to feel safe in the presence of their helper. Howard Bath, in "The Three Pillars of Trauma-Informed Care," explained:

> Ricky Greenwald, echoing the thoughts of many therapists, observes that any healing must start by creating an atmosphere of safety, and he goes on to suggest that establishing a sense of safety may take some time but formal therapy is unlikely to be successful until this critical element is in place. The notion of safety is multi-faceted and has many elements that need to be considered by care providers in addition to the more obvious needs for physical and emotional safety. For example, consistency, reliability, predictability, availability, honesty, and transparency are all attributes that are related to the creation of safe environments.

Recognize the Breadth of Functioning Impaired by Complex Trauma

You've seen that respondents to my Authoritarian Wound Questionnaire report all sorts of consequences, from physical ailments to educational and work failures to repetitive abusive relationships to feeling confused, indecisive, and "stupid," to all the classic emotional crises, like despair, high anxiety, and addiction. Consider just the wide variety of physical ailments that are sometimes attributable to trauma. Jonathan Tomlinson explained, in "We need to talk about trauma" on his blog "A Better NHS,"

> GPs like myself who have been around for long enough to develop therapeutic relationships with patients spend most of our time with patients who suffer from chronic pain, medically unexplained symptoms, addiction, eating disorders, severe obesity, self-harm, suicidal thoughts and mental health disorders; especially chronic anxiety, chronic depression, OCD, bipolar and personality disorders. Among them are our patients with the worst diabetic complications, the most symptomatic heart-failure, the most brittle asthma and out of control hypertension.
>
> They are the same patients who I met again and again as a junior doctor, who bewildered and frustrated me and my colleagues. They are still the patients who attend A&E most frequently and are most likely to fail to attend routine reviews. If they are not asking me to give them something for their chronic pain, debilitating anxiety and insomnia, for weight loss or breathlessness they need me to write reports for housing or benefits assessments. I, and thousands of doctors like me, spend every day caring for patients like this. One thing I have only very recently learned, is that Trauma is embodied.

Over time, you will gain a deep understanding of the many ways that trauma manifests. The path to that understanding begins by recognizing and accepting that past or present trauma may be contributing to or causing the difficulties that you are witnessing, whatever those difficulties may be.

Regard Issues not as Symptoms but as Human Results

Rather than conceptualizing depression as a brain disorder, addiction as a disease, hearing voices as a sign of mental illness, and in other ways analogizing from challenging human behaviors to medical conditions, begin to regard the difficulties your clients present as reactions to life experiences and as deep-seated coping mechanisms. Now that these reactions, strategies, and mechanisms have gotten tangled into personality and may even be staunchly defended by your clients, they present at the level of personality and not as mere symptom.

Your despairing client is not merely presenting despair as a symptom, he or she is a despairing human being. He or she has become this despairing person for reasons and can't very easily just "become another person." You can conceptualize your work as helping your client "travel along the road to becoming the person he or she would really like to be," rather than as symptom remediation. Your client has a long history of having had to adapt, often unsuccessfully, and having had to cope, often poorly, and you can help your client move in the direction of a "personality upgrade," which is what, maybe only in a corner of consciousness, your client really desires.

Understand Dissociative Responses

Your traumatized clients are likely also highly anxious and you will naturally work with them in the ways that you know to work with anxious clients to help them manage and reduce their anxiety. One particular anxiety reaction, dissociation, is a regular feature of the trauma picture and you will want to be alert to it, both as a clue to what your client has experienced and because it affects how your client presents in session. As Cathy Kezelman and Pam Stavropoulos write in "Practice Guidelines for the Treatment of Complex Trauma," a lengthy report funded by Australian Department of Health and Ageing:

> Understand and attune to the prevalence and varied forms of dissociative responses and the differences between hyper- and hypo-arousal. Structural dissociation represents an extreme form of defense in the face of extreme (inescapable) threat, and is a frequent feature of complex trauma when abuse begins early in childhood. Yet there are many and milder forms of dissociative response of which the therapist needs to be aware. The more you know about dissociation, the more you automatically watch for its markers. As responses to the experience of extreme anxiety, hyperarousal

is characterized by agitation, while hypo-arousal manifests as passivity, "shutting down" and withdrawal. Therapy must always remain within "the window of tolerance," that is the threshold of feeling the client can accommodate without becoming either hyper- or hypo-aroused.

Employ Special Care around Boundary Issues

Your clients who have been wounded by authoritarian contact, whether in the home, at church, at work, or somewhere else, have had their boundaries repeatedly violated. People have gotten too close to them in all the possible senses of close: too physically close, too aggressively close, too sexually close, and too much "into their business."

Kezelman and Stavropoulos explain:

> Boundaries are particularly salient with clients who have been subjected to violations, exploitations, and dual relationships. Boundaries should be mutually negotiated, and care should be taken to ensure that the client understands their significance and does not experience them as punitive. Maintenance of boundaries is also important for therapist self-care; while this is always the case, it is especially so in the demanding work of complex trauma.

As should be clear, this chapter only touches on what trauma-informed care means and looks like and only hints at how you might embrace trauma-informed care in session and in your work with clients. To repeat the main points: authoritarian wounding is traumatic and will have real consequences in the lives of your clients; trauma matters; and a field is growing that takes the importance of trauma into account and that provides recommendations for how to effectively work with traumatized clients. If you are looking for one particular orientation to pursue or one collection of ideas to examine that might help you in your work with all of your clients, victims of authoritarian wounding included, trauma-informed care might be the one.

24

EXISTENTIAL CARE

A profound way in which victims of authoritarian wounding have been harmed is that they grew up not believing that they, their concerns, or their efforts mattered. They simply didn't count. These feelings naturally and fairly inevitably led to outcomes like lifelong sadness, anxiety, suicidal thoughts, poor self-image, and an inability to live life purposefully and intentionally.

Trauma-informed care, the first line of help with regard to traumatized victims, can help with these challenges. But trauma-informed care, and any other care as well, ought to be supplemented by existential care. Any care provided to victims of authoritarian wounding ought to be supplemented with help that looks directly at encouraging clients to "return to mattering."

At the heart of existential care is the philosophy known as existentialism. Existentialism is an ambitious philosophy that demands that each human being try his or her darnedest. It begs the individual to make use of the measure of freedom he possesses, that he look life in the eye and deal with reality, and that he stand tall as an advocate for human dignity. It argues that life, by pairing tremendous ordinariness with tremendous difficulty and by leading to nothing but death, is a cheat, and that human beings must nevertheless cheat the cheater by adopting an indomitable attitude and making the meaning they require.

This agenda sets the bar very high and doesn't seem to suit most people. Existentialism failed because it is not really to most people's tastes. It makes work for them; it pesters them to be moral; it demands that they articulate their life purposes and live them; it alerts them to the likely complete purposelessness of the universe; and it announces that a kind of perpetual rebellion is necessary. That is a lot to ask.

Likewise, it trumpets that fitting in will not do and that all those easy pleasures and vices, while nobody's business but your own, still must be judged by you – and found too easy and too unethical. It keeps asserting that you must be a hero – an absurd hero, to be sure, heroically keeping meaning afloat in the face of the void and working hard at the project of your life when life itself cares nothing about your efforts. It sets the bar extremely high – too high for the vast majority of people, most existentialists included.

Existentialists themselves usually failed at living with the bar set that high. They could articulate why the bar ought to be set that high, at the place of personal responsibility and ethical action they called authentic living, but they found it inconveniently difficult to live that mindful, measured, and pure a life. They proved in the living that our foibles defeat our resolutions much of the time. They proved it by living promiscuously. They proved it by gambling. They proved it by succumbing to addiction. They proved it by giving in to despair and taking to the sofa. They proved it by rejecting real work and choosing second-rate projects. They saw clearly where they had placed the bar – apparently much too high above them.

It was simply too hard to live as carefully, ethically, and authentically as the tenets of existentialism demanded. The tenets were lovely, albeit in an ice-water sort of way, but the reality was daunting. Therefore, existentialism never really caught on. For a while after World War II millions of young people read about it, nodded in agreement with its premises, but drifted away from it because of its rigors. Jobs called; sex called; vision quests called; soccer on Saturday called; stock portfolios called. It was fine to read a little Nietzsche, Sartre, and Camus in college – but sensible, it seemed, to then put that behind you and get on with your daily commute and your evening drinking.

Existentialism didn't allow for an array of things that human beings actually wanted, like permission to be petty and permission to waste vast amounts of time. It didn't condone silent acquiescence or slogan-sized commandments. It frowned on group allegiances and social frivolity. Existential philosophy acknowledged these desires perhaps more clearly than any other philosophy but then asked people not to indulge them – and people passed on the invitation. Many remained nostalgic for those high ideals and sometimes did a little looking back, maybe reading *Nausea* or *The Stranger* in the bathroom. But essentially, they passed on the invitation, any nostalgia notwithstanding.

People passed for other reasons, too. Not only did existentialism demand that they live an ethically vigilant life where each action was the culmination of an important internal moral debate, but they were also supposed to "transcend" personality and the facts of existence and escape the net in which every human being is entangled. This was not only a lot to ask – it was perhaps unfair and impossible. How were you supposed to not be the person you had developed into? How were you supposed to shrug off illness, war, disaster, and every manner of calamity and constraint and stand tall? How, to take our main subject, were you supposed to transcend the real victimization you experienced at the hands of an authoritarian? How was any of that really doable?

Take human energy itself. The existential vision pictures a human being in control of herself. But what if you are flying along in a manic way in pursuit of some impossible dream and really don't want to stop and take a measured reckoning? What if you want to act impulsively – intuitively, if you like – and take a pass on some stolid calm that seriously slows you down? It seemed like a choice had to be made between a snail's pace rationality and our very life force – and people choose pulsation over calculation.

To be fair, many existentialists understood all this. Each danced the poignant dance of demanding much from human beings while doubting that the effort was possible or even plausible. They doubted and wondered. Why make such a Herculean effort at authenticity when personality hung like a lead weight around your neck and the facts of existence ruined many of your plans? All that wondering and doubting lead to those trademarks of existential thought: fear and trembling, nausea, existential anxiety, existential dread and, of course, absurdity.

The more we announced that man mattered, the more we saw that he really didn't. The better we understood that the dinosaurs could be extinguished in the blink of an eye by an asteroid strike or some other natural disaster, the better we understood that we could suffer a similar fate. The better we understood the power of microbes, and even as we worked hard and pretty well to fight them, the better we understood that something functionally invisible and endlessly prevalent could end our personal journey on any given afternoon. The more science taught us, the more we shrank in size – and shrank back in horror. You could build the largest particle accelerator the world had ever seen and recreate the Big Bang and psychologically speaking you would end up with only more of nothing – *even* more of nothing, if that were possible.

It is this apprehension of cosmic indifference that existentialists faced squarely – and demanded that you face, too. But who wants that daily dose of despair? We had all somehow wagered that well-stocked supermarkets and guaranteed elections would do the trick and protect us from the void. But they didn't. This now 100-year-long *certainty* that we are throwaways has made life look completely unfunny. We can laugh together over a bottle of wine and make small talk about this and that, adding a kind of cultural laugh track to a very unfunny situation comedy. But in most of our private seconds there is not much laughter. Rather there is a deep, wide, abiding "Why bother?" And who wanted existentialists reminding us of *that*?

Still, existential ideals are probably the right ones. You take as much control as possible of your thoughts, your attitudes, your moods, your behaviors, and your very orientation toward life and marshal your innate freedom in the service of your intentions. You stand up, you tell truth to power, you name and then take responsibility for your life purpose choices, you deal with meaninglessness by making new meaning investments and seizing new meaning opportunities, and you dismiss absurdity as true but irrelevant. This is quite a mouthful – and not for everyone. But is it perhaps for you? And is it perhaps what will most help your clients who have been wounded by their contact with an authoritarian and who do not feel as if they count or matter?

How might you add an existential component to your helping? It's simple enough. You begin by listening. You start to conjure responses in your own mind. You ask questions for clarification, if you do not understand. At some point, you decide where you want to focus and how you want to reply. All helpers do this. The difference is that you include wonders about meaning, life purpose, and the other large "existential" issues of life in your thinking and in your speculating. There are many ways to conceptualize this work, but one way is to suppose that you are helping clients in nine specific areas. You can present this to clients as "nine steps to personal fulfillment" or "nine ways to live with more purpose" or in any language you like. Or, rather than presenting it to them, you can use this list to inform your work with clients.

Here is what you are inviting clients to do:

You Decide to Matter

The universe is not built to care about you. You must care about you. You must announce that you are opting to matter. You must announce that you are making the startling, eye-opening decision to take responsibility for your thoughts and your actions and live life instrumentally.

You Accept That You Must Make Meaning

You finally let go of the demoralizing wish that meaning rain down on you from some golden universal shower and accept that the only meaning that exists is the meaning that you make. You announce once and for all that you are the final arbiter of meaning.

You Identify Your Life Purposes

If you are going to actively make meaning in accordance with your life purposes, you had better know what your life purposes are, articulate them, memorize them, and make sure that you really believe in them.

You Articulate a Life Purpose Statement

You list your life purposes, rank order your life purposes, and do something with them that allows you to hold in a single phrase or a single sentence a clear understanding of how you intend to live your life and represent yourself in the universe.

You Hold the Intention to Fulfill Your Life Purposes

You need to keep your meaning-making efforts firmly in mind. You must be able to remember your life purposes even when you are tired, bothered, distracted, upset, and otherwise not in your best frame of mind. When life resumes it habitual busyness, you are still able to firmly hold your intentions and manifest them.

You Passionately Act to Fulfill Your Life Purposes

Every day you make some meaning in accordance with your life purposes. Maybe eight hours of your day are robbed by activities that do not align with your life purposes and that you must attend to for all the usual reasons. But some hours remain – and you must use them!

You Navigate the World and the Facts of Existence

The world is not built to accommodate you. Your favorite bakery may close or war may break out – from the smallest to the largest, the facts of existence are exactly what they are. They include pain and pleasure, loyalty and betrayal, life and death. All this you must navigate, right up until the final moment.

You Create Yourself in Your Own Best Image

You have indubitable strengths and every manner of shadow. If you live in those shadows you will never quite respect yourself. Do better by manifesting your strengths and becoming the person you know you want to become. Surrender to the truth that you would prefer to be your best self.

You Live the Life of a Passionate Meaning-Maker

You don't idly chat about meaning, brood about meaning, look for meaning, complain about meaning, buy a book about meaning, take a workshop on meaning: you make meaning. You live a life where, day in and day out, you make meaning. You make choices, decisions, and an effort. You wait on nothing: you live.

What flows from embracing these precepts, if a client is willing, is a way of negotiating each day so that he or she gets to live his or her newly-articulated life purposes. Existential-informed care involves helping clients make decisions about "how much meaning they need," where they will make that meaning, when they'll feel entitled to "vacations from meaning," and so on. This is a way of conceptualizing how to turn the idea of "living intentionally" into a genuine daily practice.

When you live your life as a passionate meaning-maker each day is a special sort of negotiation. You make decisions about where you will invest meaning and how you will handle activities that hold no particular meaning for you. You make a daily bargain with yourself that if you hold to your intentions you will find no reason to doubt the meaningfulness of that day. It is like saying, "If I have a good breakfast, somehow get through the holiday buffet at the office without overdoing it, and have just one treat this evening, I won't get down on myself about what I ate today."

You do not aim for some unattainable perfection. You recognize that the three hours you spend making phone calls to nursing homes on behalf of your ailing father should be toted up on the side of meaning, even if they feel like drudgery and even if the actual phoning makes you anxious. You accept that you need vacations from "the whole meaning thing" on a daily basis and pencil in the novel you want to read or the movie you want to watch without the slightest pang of guilt. At the same time, you adamantly demand of yourself that you put in that hard hour on your Internet business doing the thing that you've been avoiding doing. This is not a "perfect" day as measured against some imaginary ideal, but it is a carefully negotiated day full of hard work, service, and relaxation and a day to completely accept – and to be proud of.

All day long you make judgments and decisions, judging, for instance, that a moment has come when you *had better* make some meaning or else risk a meaning crisis; or deciding that plenty of meaning has been made already, and that now you're entitled to a television show and some chocolate. You use your various techniques, like maintaining a morning meaning practice, to effectively negotiate your daily meaning challenges. These are the sorts of ideas that an existentially inclined helper can share with clients. Over time, such a helper will acquire all sorts of useful tactics and strategies and find his or her idiosyncratic ways of helping clients deal more effectively with their doubts and fears that they matter and their challenges in the realms of life purpose and meaning.

25

INTERPERSONAL, RELATIONAL, AND FAMILY HELP

Authoritarian wounding is an interpersonal matter. The victim isn't just thinking something or feeling something: something traumatic happened to him or her at the hands of another person.

Since victims have been harmed by some particular actual human being or human beings, it makes sense that they will have troubles in their relationships with other human beings and maybe even in their relationships with all human beings, including you.

It is logical to suppose that victims of authoritarian wounding will have problems relating. Therefore, helping them improve their relationships, helping them better understand family dynamics, and helping them gain basic relationship skills are worthy goals as you picture how you and your wounded clients might work together.

A simple and effective way to help clients in these areas is to focus on two qualities, strength and bravery. In my work as a family therapist, I've found that inviting clients to manifest new strength and new courage resonates for them. They may not be quite equal to the task, but the idea makes sense to them and strikes them as a worthy if not immediately attainable goal. You may find that this way of working suits you, too.

Why focus on strength? Because living in most families and engaging in any sort of intimate relationship requires a lot of fortitude, stamina, and strength. Being criticized over and over again is more wearing and more tiring than a long march.

Feeling abandoned, misunderstood, or rejected is harder on the system than climbing a mountain. We need great strength to say what we mean, if saying what we mean feels threatening and comes with a history of retaliation. We need great strength to deal with a mate who envies our success, a parent who snickers at our life choices, or a child who requires our constant attention. Family life is nothing if not demanding.

This is not a strength that we can acquire in the gym (though being healthy and fit is certainly a good thing). This is an internal fortitude that we must muster and manifest. This looks like us instantly disputing self-talk like "I can't do that" with a firm "Yes, I can!" When I work with the clients I coach, we often spend a lot of time focusing on mustering and manifesting this strength. One of the ways we do that is by rehearsing and role-playing. Often what's required before a person can manifest her strength is rehearsing what she intends to say, visualizing the interaction in all its details, and picturing the possibly negative consequences. If rehearsing and role-playing are congenial to you, this is a sort of work that you can do to help clients build inner fortitude.

One client hated it that her husband would not follow through on a "simple" household project. Their downstairs bathroom needed a new toilet and her husband had gotten as far as removing the old toilet, sitting it in the living room, and stopping there. That old toilet now sat in her living room and had sat there for months. Not only was it an eyesore and not only did it prevent her from socializing in her own home, it was living proof of the difficulties she was having in her marriage and a living reproach that screamed at her, "You are so weak!" It took all her strength to give her husband the ultimatum that this toilet in the living room was a marriage deal breaker. Even with that ultimatum, he still took his sweet time finishing the downstairs bathroom remodel – but at least a day did come when the old toilet finally left the living room.

Another client found that she was being held hostage by her mother's will. She had turned over her life to caretaking her aged mother and each time she tried to discuss the possibility that some other arrangement had to be made so that she, the daughter, could have a life, her mother would threaten to remove her from her will. This threat had worked for many years. It took us some time to discern what concrete "strength" she needed to muster in order to free herself from the grip of that dangled legacy. Finally, we came upon it: she needed to buy a plane ticket to the place she intended to relocate. With that ticket in hand, she was able to have the conversation with her mother that she had needed to have for so long, one that she now felt strong enough to engage in no matter what her mother threatened about beneficiaries and bequests.

A third client needed to find the strength to continue with her writing career even though her husband had grown very envious of her success. He craved the income she produced but also belittled her efforts, which had caused her to block and stop writing. She came to me not understanding why she wasn't writing, given that she loved writing, felt connected to her current writing project, and had readers waiting for her next book. It quickly became clear that her husband's passive-aggressive attitude toward her success had somehow crept into her psyche and caused her to block.

In her case, the strength that she had to muster was the not inconsiderable strength it takes to live with a passive-aggressive mate. She had to tune him out, she had to call him on his behaviors (like filling up her writing study with "things that we don't have room for in the garage"), and she had to speak to him clearly and directly about not belittling her readers, her genre, or her efforts.

A fourth client had to find the strength to send her teenager away to a therapeutic wilderness camp despite his loud unwillingness to go. For several years he'd been declining, doing progressively more poorly in school, picking up a drug and alcohol habit, and finally, as a last straw, dealing drugs. Now the law had gotten involved – and even that drama did not seem to wake her son up to his predicament. My client held this wilderness camp as her last hope and it took mustering all her strength to demand that he go, despite his violent protestations and self-harm threats. In fact, the wilderness camp experience seemed to turn his life around – which is often the sort of blessing a person receives when she is able to manifest her strength within her troubled family.

Very often, we live as a weakened version of ourselves because life has beaten us down, because we've failed too many times and no longer trust ourselves to succeed, because we have trouble holding a clear vision of our life purposes and our most important intentions, or for some other reason or combination of reasons. Of course, one of those reasons for the clients we've been discussing will be the authoritarian wounding they've experienced. I hope that the above examples give you a taste of what "working on strength" might look like with your clients.

And what about working on bravery? Bravery is of course a cousin to strength. Sometimes we feel weak. Then we need to manifest our strength. Other times we feel afraid. Then we need to manifest our courage. Many people feel afraid inside their own family. The fear may arise because they are physically abused or verbally abused. The fear may arise because they feel like they have to walk on eggshells or else provoke criticism or an outburst. So, they move through their house – and their life – silently and stealthily. Sometimes the fear is rather hard to ferret out, as it was with the following client.

I had a client who, as it turned out after we had explored many other avenues, was afraid to come home from work. He wasn't physically afraid of his wife – it was nothing like that. What he feared was realizing all over again that he didn't love her or even like her, that they weren't suited to be together, and that sooner or later, and despite the fact that they had two small children, they would have to divorce. It may seem odd to call this "fear," but that's exactly what it felt like to my client. The prospect of going home each day – or rather, the prospect of what he would realize the instant he stepped inside the door – terrified him.

When we began working together he had no inkling that he was challenged in this way. He described his problems in other ways: that he was a workaholic who put in the most hours of any lawyer at his law firm; that he was overly obsessed with fitness and as a result spent too many hours at the gym, thus "neglecting his home life"; that, like so many of his fellow lawyers, he had great difficulty "balancing work and family"; and that he had "trouble making and keeping friends," which problem he had made an effort to solve by setting up frequent after-work social events at one or another local watering hole.

Nowhere in the presentation of his perceived difficulties was there a hint of any fear of going home – or any hint of fear at all. Yet after several sessions it became clear to both of us that not only did he hate going home, he actually feared going home. He could feel the anxiety and fear well up in him as the day progressed and as quitting time approached. To deal with that fear he would keep working and stay as late as possible at the office; or he would leave work and go to a bar and socialize; or he would leave work and go directly to the gym. This new knowledge shed a bright light on his "troublesome" behaviors, putting them in their proper context.

Once he understood what was going on, he then had to face it. He had to face the fact that he hated his marriage and that it terrified him to own up to that truth. We worked on him manifesting his courage in two specific ways. First, he had to bravely go home at an appropriate time every day, if for no other reason than that his children needed him to be a parent. Second, he had to bravely broach the "our marriage isn't working" subject with his wife – as well as broaching it more fully with himself.

Neither proved easy. He found it hard to go home at an appropriate time because, to name one of his reasons, "My annual review is approaching and my bonus hinges on how many hours I put in." Likewise, he found it hard to muster the courage to look at the prospect of his marriage actually ending. Manifesting that courage in both ways became the work of our next couple of months together and he ultimately succeeded in the arriving at the next logical step of his journey, which was couples' counseling.

Your clients may have the same sort of trouble knowing that something is frightening them. An adolescent may have framed her reluctance to come home from school as annoyance at the long walk home rather than as fear of coming home to an empty, too-quiet house. Your work-from-home client may have named his inability to get work done at home as his "attention deficit disorder" rather than as his fear of asking family members to be quiet. Given that fear may not be presented, how can you come to know that your client is frightened of something if he or she doesn't currently have access to that knowledge? One way is to ask them the following question: "Might there be something that you're afraid of that you don't know that you're afraid of?" That's one effective starting point.

And if you learn that fear is at play? One tactic, exercise, or "enactment" that I use is the following one. You might think about trying it out. Place two scatter rugs (or their equivalent) a few inches apart. Have your client stand at the edge of one of them, facing the other one. Provide the following verbal cues: "Imagine that you are standing at the edge of a cliff with a deep gorge between you and the other cliff. Feel the depth of that gorge and how terrifying it would be to fall down it. But, as deep and as frightening as that gorge is, it only takes a small step to cross it. Take that small step across while at the same thinking 'Many fears are like this.' Feel the deep comfort of arriving safely on the other side!"

After your client has crossed (or not crossed) to the other side, process his reaction to the exercise.

Being strong and being brave can manifest in all sorts of ways. For one client, it will be staying in a currently unacceptable relationship but staying in new safer or stronger ways; for another client, it will be leaving the relationship. It may take the form of saying something that scares your client to say, making a hard decision that terrifies your client to contemplate, or penetrating his defenses and looking courageously at something that frightens him to see. It may mean losing financial security or it may mean the complete uprooting of your client's life.

The headlines from this chapter are that you can expect your clients who have been wounded by authoritarian contact to have relationship issues (like the compulsion to choose one authoritarian mate after another, as we saw in an earlier chapter) and that you can work on these issues in ways as simple as focusing on qualities like strength and courage. Of course, there are all sorts of other ways that you might work on these issues as well. Do expect these relationship issues to be coming: they almost surely are. Whether or not you are technically a couples' counselor, family therapist, or relationship expert, acquiring skills in these areas will prove of great service to your clients.

26

TIPS FOR DEALING WITH AN AUTHORITARIAN PARENT

Authoritarian wounding comes primarily at the hands of two groups of authoritarians, parents and mates. Of course, the authoritarian in a given client's life might be (or might have been) his or her grandparent, uncle or aunt, sibling, boss, pastor, or even his or her own child. But most usually, the authoritarian was (or is) a parent or mate. That's why we're focusing on parents in this chapter and mates in the next.

Your client may be in his or her 30s, 40s, or 50s; that is, he or she may be an adult with a family of his or her own and may still be dealing with an authoritarian parent who is likely in his or her 50s, 60s, 70s, 80s, or older. The following are some suggestions that you can make to a client who finds himself or herself in that position, if you offer suggestions, or avenues that you can explore with your client, if you engage in such explorations.

Creating Physical Separation

Virtually all respondents reported that only physical separation, and the wider the separation the better, allowed them to feel safe and provided them with the opportunity to heal. Because this was reported so often and was so regularly presented as the only thing that worked for them, we'll spend a whole chapter on the subject of guilt-free physical separation. A headline is that you would love clients to live with that separation with as little guilt as possible. You can remind them that safety needs come first and likewise remind them of the extent to which the authoritarian forced this separation by his or her behaviors. You can also underline that they are not alone in the decision they made: most victims of authoritarian wounding come to the same conclusion.

Creating Psychological Separation

Children can't help but get enmeshed with their parents and continue, often for their whole lives, to be affected by their parents' behaviors and attitudes. They are also likely to still love (or feel that they ought to love) their parents, to be pressured by other family members to continue to deal, psychologically and emotionally, with their parents, and to never quite be able to get their parents out of their head.

As respondent Mark put it,

> Both of my parents have been dead for more than ten years and I'm still not free of them. I still rage at them internally; I keep telling them what they did to me; they keep denying it and keep shaming me; and all of this is going on in my own head. This is all my own doing now. Meditation hasn't helped; CBT hasn't helped; I feel like I need some kind of surgery. The only thing that helps is drugs – and I know that can't be the right answer.

Calling Parents on Their Attitudes and Behaviors

Many respondents discovered that saying some variation of "No!" and "That's not okay!" caused the authoritarian parent to moderate, modulate, or even stop his or her behaviors.

To take one example, respondent Alice explained,

> My mother always screamed at me. So, I would try to find some summer camp to attend just to get away from home. It didn't matter what the camp was offering – music, swimming, whatever – I would go. One summer when I was about twelve I went to a camp that had these "talking sessions" – I guess it was actually some sort of group therapy or encounter group or peer counseling, I don't know what. I found myself telling my story. A boy I kind of liked blurted out, "Scream back!" When I got back home I did just that. My mother started screaming at the mess I'd made of my clothes and I got into her face and shouted, "Stop screaming at me!" And she did! And the screaming stopped. It was like she woke up from a trance."

Many clients will have had a different experience; sometimes calling out an authoritarian only increases the punishment. You will want to keep this in mind: that the outcome of calling out an authoritarian may be remarkably positive, or it may be dangerous and provocative. You might profitably discuss the pros and cons of taking an action of this sort with a client who is contemplating it.

Exorcising Guilt and Shame

Respondents expressed all sorts of guilt. Some felt guilty about not protecting their younger siblings from the family authoritarian. Some felt guilty about having failed themselves or not living up to their potential. Some felt guilty about physically or emotionally separating from their authoritarian parent. Some felt guilty about having contributed to their own physical problems by not doing a better job of healing their psychological wounds. Likewise, and for similar reasons, many felt ashamed of themselves as well as guilty.

Respondent Maryanne explained,

> I kept hearing myself say, "I should go see dad; after all, he is my dad." But it scared me to see him and I knew better than to see him. So, I never went – and I felt tremendously guilty about that. Then I began working with a cognitive-behavioral therapist. I really didn't believe that CBT could possibly go deep enough; I had the prejudice that it was a shallow kind of thing. But as I got into the habit of actually substituting a thought I wanted to think for the constant "I should see dad," I began to stop thinking that thought and the guilt kind of melted away. I'm guessing that not everybody gets that lucky, but I did!

Testing Careful Compassion

Some respondents felt compassion for the authoritarian in question, expressing that the authoritarian parent had himself or herself suffered gravely in childhood. These respondents sometimes came to the conclusion that a little compassion might not be a dangerous thing; and some went on to reach out to the authoritarian parent in the hopes of reconnecting with him or her and heal the relationship.

Many of these efforts ended unsuccessfully, with the authoritarian taking the gesture as a new opportunity to shame and punish. However, a few efforts turned out well. That a few efforts did turn out well suggests that if your client is contemplating an effort of this sort, you can be carefully encouraging, perhaps by helping your client see the potential pitfalls and downside while at the same agreeing that the risks involved might just be worth it.

Creating a Support System

Your client who has been wounded by an authoritarian parent has been subjected to traumatic experiences with lifelong consequences. He or she likely needs additional support, in addition to the support you are offering him or her. This support might include anything from a 12-step program to a peer support group to a dear friend to a sympathetic hairdresser. You might bring this up with clients via the question, "Is there any additional support you think you need, in addition to meeting with me?" Your client may say no or he or she may say yes; and if he or she says yes, that will likely lead to a conversation as to what that support might look like and where it might come from.

Respondent Maria explained,

> I have to be able to handle things on my own, because, growing up, I lost so much power and so much self-confidence that my goal for myself is be powerful and self-confident. But that I want to handle things on my own doesn't mean that I have to be completely on my own or handle every single thing alone. So, I've created a kind of informal support team. I don't turn to them first thing – first, I want to trust my own resources. But I'm not stubborn, and I do turn to them just as soon as I understand that I could use some help!

Staying Alert for Triggers

In the language of the 12-step recovery movement, a trigger is an internal or external cue that is likely to cause a person in recovery to relapse and resume the addictive behavior. A trigger might be the appearance of a certain feeling, like feeling overwhelmed, being yelled at, criticized, shamed, or punished, seeing someone in a film or a television show in a situation like yours, relationship events that mimic family-of-origin events, or even encountering a certain smell (like an aftershave lotion) or a certain sound (like a door slamming).

You can help clients decide what they will do if some triggering event occurs. They might decide that they will contact a support person, take a walk or exercise, employ self-talk that reminds them of their intentions (say, of their intention not to go to a place of shame or guilt), meditate, or engage in some deep breathing. As respondent Marvin explained,

> I used street drugs to deal with my feelings of worthlessness that were a product of growing up with a really mean, shaming dad. Once I entered recovery, I had to figure out what my triggers were – one sneaky one was seeing some man wearing a knit cap like my father used to wear – and knowing exactly what to do when a trigger occurred.

Communicating with and Enlisting "Healthy" or "Sane" Family Members

Many respondents expressed how maintaining contact with family members who saw the situation the same way that they did was their number-one healing and survival strategy. A client and her sisters might support one another in validating their memories ("Yes, Anna, it *was* that bad!"), standing together in mutual defense and in ongoing defiance of the authoritarian parent, and sometimes even finding ways of seeing humor among the horrors.

Respondent Jennifer explained,

> When I try to go it alone, I can't deal with my mother. But when I'm with my sisters, the whole thing seems less tragic. I

think that's why we live close to one another; that very proximity is a kind of armor against mom's assaults. I remember when I had to go see mom on a piece of legal business. I was so dreading it I was making myself sick. Finally, my sisters both announced, "We're coming with you!" They did; I survived; and their company – I would say, protection – made all the difference in the world.

Not Accepting the Vision of Siblings or Other Family Members Who Do Not See the Situation as You See It

Other family members may have had a very different experience of mom and dad from your client's experience. This may have occurred for any number of reasons. They may have entered the family later than your client; maybe the authoritarian had mellowed by that time and your client's much younger sisters and brothers did not receive the same authoritarian wounding as your client did. Maybe your client was less favored than his or her siblings and singled out for shaming and punishment. Maybe your client's siblings were in fact just as abused and traumatized as your client was, but they are currently in denial about their experiences or have followed in the authoritarian's footsteps. If any of this is the case, your client will need to defend himself or herself against their contrary vision, their demands that your client "be nicer" to the authoritarian parent, and their accusations that your client is being disloyal or ungrateful.

Respondent Alfred explained,

> I'm one of three brothers. The eldest is just like our father. He's a complete bully. I can deal with him because I know exactly who he is. My younger brother is convinced that nothing bad ever happened in our house. When I say to him, "Do you remember when dad busted the door to the shed?" or "Do you remember when dad took Bobby out and beat him?" he looks at me like I'm insane. That's so hard to deal with! Part of me needs him to remember and needs him to corroborate my understanding of what happened. And I know that's never going to happen. That makes me very sad.

Limiting Contact

Your client may still be living with his or her authoritarian parent or may have returned to live with that parent, perhaps because the parent has become infirm. For that client, complete physical separation is out of the question and complete psychological separation is unlikely. For a client in this position, you might pose a question like "What's the least amount of contact you can have with your mom?" or "How might you stay out of your dad's way most of the time?" and see how your client reacts to your suggestion about limiting contact.

What might it look like to limit contact? Respondent Amelia explained,

> I moved back into the family house to take care of my mother when none of my siblings were willing to even lend a hand. I hated that I let myself guilt-trip myself into doing that but I also loved my mother, so it was a complicated moment. But what I did was only see my mother when I absolutely had to. I was otherwise really unavailable. I chose a room in the house far away from my mother, I went out a lot, and, most importantly, I made it clear to myself that I didn't need to "keep her company" – because "keeping her company" was inevitably toxic.

It may not be your style of helping to provide tips or to offer suggestions. Nevertheless, I hope that you can find ways to make use of the above ten tips in your work with wounded clients, perhaps simply by keeping them in a corner of consciousness and strategically nodding when a client comes to one of these realizations on his or her own. Personally, I am for a directive way of working that allows for suggestions (which is one reason I now work as a coach rather than as a therapist, which I used to do). Whether your way is directive or nondirective, I hope these tips serve you.

27

SUPPORTING PHYSICAL AND EMOTIONAL SEPARATION

Your client may still be living with or dealing with the authoritarian in his or her life. That will pose real, ongoing challenges for your client. Unfortunately, there are no wonderful answers for a person in that position and no single tactic or strategy that is sure to work for every client. That's one reason why you can prove so valuable; you can help your client create a plan that best suits his or her circumstances.

To repeat, there's no "magic bullet" tactic that will work for every client. For example, many respondents explained how standing up to the authoritarian for the first time radically reduced the authoritarian's harmful behaviors. However, other respondents who tried to stand their ground were severely punished for their efforts. So, we can't assert as a rule, "Always stand up to authoritarians" or "Never stand up to authoritarians." For one of your clients, standing up might prove exactly the right thing for him or her to do, and for another client, the consequences of a courageous act of that sort might prove dire.

The headline is that there isn't a one-size-fits-all solution. That is the message you will want to communicate to clients. Each client will have to navigate the situation without guarantees and without even a decent roadmap. However, one strategy did seem to work well for almost all respondents who tried it: physically separating from the authoritarian in question. The further the distance, the safer the respondent felt. The less contact with the authoritarian, the more that healing tended to occur. For many respondents, staying far away and never seeing the authoritarian again were the only strategies that really helped them.

The dynamics were different depending on whether the authoritarian in question was a parent or a mate. More so when it came to parents than to mates, if the respondent managed such a separation he or she often felt guilty as a result. The cognition accompanying the guilt was usually of the "I should love my parent no matter what" or "I know my parent had a terrible time of it, so isn't forgiveness the way to go?" variety. The guilt generated by thoughts of this sort was typically powerful and persistent, often so powerful and persistent as to "force" the respondent to reach out to the parent in question – usually with unsatisfactory, triggering results that undid much of the healing.

When it came to mates rather than to parents, respondents who managed such a separation rarely felt guilty for leaving. But they did typically experience considerable shame for having stayed for so long with an abusive, unsuitable person who not only inflicted harm on the respondent but also on any children in the picture. Respondents simply could not understand why they stayed with an abusive mate for five, ten, fifteen, twenty, or more years, or why, having broken free from one such mate, they then went on to pick another abusive mate, and then another. They found their own behavior both incomprehensible and deeply shameful.

To repeat this headline, respondents typically felt guilty about completely separating from an authoritarian parent and ashamed about staying so long with an authoritarian mate. You can help your client who has managed to separate from the authoritarian in his or her life not feel so guilty about the action he or she took and not so ashamed about the actions he or she failed to take. These are areas of potentially wonderful healing, areas that if addressed will make a real difference in your client's life.

Many of these physical separations proved hugely successful. Respondent Elizabeth described the benefits of physical separation in the following way:

> I think we all (my mother and three sisters) lived in fear of my father. It was the 50s and early 60s – the Mad Men era – and we were all dependent on my dad's income. I was born in 1955. My father was an Air Force pilot, alcoholic, perfectionist,

artist, cook, and voracious learner. I had tremendous admiration for him, but a deep resentment of his drinking and his iron hand, which he exhibited almost exclusively when he drank. When he wasn't drinking, he could be jovial, playful, and fun to be around. But when he drank …

I couldn't wait to leave home and go away to college. I definitely felt happier on my own. I never felt unsafe at home – more like oppressed. I was always the responsible, studious child, so going away to college was an extension of my explorations and getting the space I needed to be my own authority. Getting away helped me and allowed me to grow into a self-reliant person. Nowadays I avoid authoritarian people like the plague. At my ripe old age, when I find myself around them, I take a secret pleasure in calling them out. It feels very liberating to speak in my own voice, a voice that I managed to cultivate because I escaped my home.

The authoritarian may not be a parent or a mate. For example, the dynamics of gaining physical separation from a sibling possess their own unique complexities. Regina explained:

My sister is nine years older than me. From the time I was born, I think my sister disliked me or maybe was jealous of me. Maybe sibling rivalry to the max! She was always very critical of me, bossy, bullying and demeaning to me. She had many character traits of this sort and treated everyone with a heavy hand but I was a sensitive child and am now an HSP (Highly Sensitive Person) and just "took it" harder than the average person.

I think my sister was an "authoritarian leader" as she had to be the center of attention all the time. She had a big ego and loved to make fun of others, put the weaker or disabled down and make herself feel more important. From childhood, I knew this was wrong. Her behavior never stopped – throughout our lives she continued belittling others, pumping herself up and, like the vulture she was, soaring down and making mincemeat out of her "prey."

She ran for many offices and won, too, starting with social chair of her high school student council and eventually becoming the mayor of her town (several times). She loved to lead. More than that, though, she loved power and control (all with maybe a touch of sadism), just like many politicians these days do, too. Our middle sister once said that she was the type who would pull the wings off a butterfly.

So, I distanced myself from her, called her names as a child, and now I have severed all ties with her (for the past six years). I am okay with this choice. I feel better! I feel lighter, saner, less judged and less criticized. However, this sister has two adult daughters who she turned against me, and I lost them and my three grandnieces and my grandnephew in the departure, too. That hurt.

My advice? Walk away. Walk away at any and all costs. STOP interacting with the person who hurt you. Life goes on and so will you – you'll be happier, healthier, saner and smarter, too. Life's hard enough as it is. You don't need anyone judging, criticizing or demeaning you. EVER! Let go of this person or persons and live lighter, better and more joyfully. I did and I have some sadness but no regrets. Life is to enjoy!

It may come as a surprise how often the required separation is from a sibling. Respondent Denise provided another sibling story:

My mother was very strict with me and so was my older sister, who constantly criticized me about everything – my appearance, my behavior and so forth. My mother tried to scare me with religious notions because she thought me to be a "bad girl" for not following everything she wanted me to do. My authoritarian sister fueled the flames by telling lies to my mother, such as saying I had taken drugs as a teen when I never did. My mother always believed my sister and not me.

When I did chores as a child such as washing the floor, my mother always insisted I do it again as it was not good enough. My sister was held up to me as the epitome of womanhood, married with three children and who did not work outside the home. Also, my sister was very religious. I was thoroughly sick of the criticism, religious threats and undermining of my identity by my mother and particularly by my sister. I couldn't "talk back" as my mother would not allow it, but I rebelled by going out.

As an adult, I decided to "divorce" my sister as I could not tolerate the game-playing. For example, my mother would go to my sister's home for an occasion, such as Thanksgiving, and call me the next day telling me what a nice time they had and about all the home-cooked food and so forth. I was not invited to my niece's wedding as my sister only wanted "close family" at the event. Her kids were not to call me auntie, but my sister's friend was called auntie.

I am happy not to have contact with my sister anymore. But when I meet people, they always ask me about my siblings, so I feel uncomfortable, and I don't want to tell my whole story. Few would believe how mean my sister was to me, as she looks like the perfect housewife and mother. But I know. And I know that a complete separation from her was necessary.

There is also the idea of physical separation from an institution. Respondent Leslie explained:

There were at least three major authoritarians in my life, my dad, my husband, and the Catholic Church. I had an alcoholic father who fluctuated among silence, irritation, rage, and amazing storytelling. I was raised as a Catholic and the patriarchy there was pretty extreme. I found myself acquiescing to the demands of whoever was in charge without much thought.

There was a definite hierarchy in the church. The priest was revered and obeyed in his parish but he was subservient to the bishops, cardinals, and the pope. The nuns were pretty much subservient, period, although the Mother Superior had some power over the other nuns. But she always acquiesced to the priest. From all of this, I became a first class, well-trained, very adaptive enabler. I learned that everyone else's needs were more important than mine. And I learned that I should be grateful that I could help all those who needed my assistance in any way.

That made me a very good teacher and wife and friend to all except myself. I learned to not push back. The exception to that was if I needed to defend or protect someone else. Then I could speak up with authority and power. Unfortunately, it took a series of life traumas (betrayal, divorce, cancer) to open my eyes and give me the courage to have authority over myself and trust in me.

Years of therapy helped, as did 12-step work, lots of women's groups, and fostering my creativity. And careful separation helped. Not complete separation from the Church: I still have many friendships with priests and I teach at a Catholic university. But I am no longer a practicing Catholic. Nor did I completely separate from my dad: my dad passed away but we resolved our relationship before he died. But with my authoritarian ex I have NO contact whatsoever. It is the only way, because any contact with him is toxic. I feel free, safer, and happier nowadays, and my creativity knows no bounds.

So far, we've been chatting about physical separation. Important, too, is psychological or emotional separation: getting the authoritarian out of your head. When clients can't pull off physical separation, say because they are still at home under their parents' roof, still with their mate, or still at a job they can't afford to leave, then an important tactic is trying to gain psychological or emotional separation. Respondent Maria, for example, made the following clear distinction:

My father and I made a complete break of our relationship when I was 12 years old. We coexisted until I was about 24, when I graduated from college. Then my parents divorced and he moved out. I felt safer and saner making a complete break from him and the only regret I have is never having had a father, as I see others have.

As for my current authoritarian boss, I have not yet made a complete break, as I need the job and I am 19 months from retirement and 12 months from her retirement. But who's counting? I am civil to her in the office, and I speak to her only when I'm required to do so. Although she is more pleasant towards me since I reported her to HR, I will never allow myself to forget how she has treated me, and I would never want any type of a relationship with her that wasn't work-based. Once the job is over, that relationship will end neatly and completely.

As for my boss, the greatest coping technique has been emotional detachment. I take nothing she says or does personally. I recognize that I have greater goals in my life and that this is a paycheck for now. This job does not define who I am, but only what I am doing at this time in my life. I have made very concrete plans of what I will do when I am able to retire from this position and each day I keep those plans as my main focus and nothing she can do will deter me from succeeding at those plans.

To repeat this headline, when a client either isn't equal to physically separating or has his or her reasons for not physically separating, then emotional or psychological separation may be the "next best thing." These are areas where helpers can prove really valuable. You can help clients deal with the guilt of physically separating from an authoritarian parent, the shame of staying too long with an authoritarian mate, and the complicated dynamics of separating from institutions like the church or from relatives like siblings. Likewise, you can help them gain psychological and emotional separation where physical separation is not currently a possibility. You have a lot of help to offer in these areas!

28

MY 15 LEARNINGS

When I began my research, I presumed that there must be a lot of authoritarian wounding out there, given how toxic growing up with or living with an authoritarian personality had to be and given how many authoritarians are among us. When, as history has shown us repeatedly, whole populations look primed to follow a fascist leader, and given the authoritarian research conducted by Adorno, Altemeyer, and others, I supposed that it must be the case that within the family – within a great many families – this same dynamic must be playing itself out in microcosm, harming millions, many if not most permanently.

This is indeed what I found. I also learned all of the following, some of which surprised me at first glance – but not at second glance. I hope that these observations help complete the picture I've been painting of authoritarian wounding and what can be done to help the victims of authoritarian wounding heal and cope.

1 Most of the respondents were female. I could speculate as to why this is the case, but it would only be speculation. It might be that men are trained not to share embarrassing or shameful experiences; it might be that boys who experience authoritarian contact tend to grow up to become authoritarians themselves and so would never respond to a questionnaire like mine. I have no answers as to why this is the case, but it does mirror the reality that women make up the majority of therapy clients and coaching clients as

well as the majority of participants at workshops geared toward growth, healing, and emotional health.

2 The men who did respond reported the same sorts of consequences as did the women. All of the consequences I've described previously, including depression, anxiety, addiction, physical complaints, repetition compulsions, work and family failures, indecisiveness and confusion, and so on, were reported by the men who responded to my Authoritarian Wound Questionnaire as well as by the women. This suggests that there is one "typical" outcome (or outcome picture). It would be fascinating to see more research into this "typical" outcome picture.

3 Respondents were not professional writers or storytellers and yet their stories were not just homespun and real but also eloquent. This suggests that a narrative approach to healing might prove a go-to strategy for some helpers. Asking clients to write their story, either in response to questions or in response to some other sort of prompt, gives clients a chance, maybe the first chance they have ever been offered or have ever afforded themselves, to get clear on the extent to which they were harmed and to gain insight into their own difficulties, behaviors, and personality. Most respondents reported that they found responding to the Authoritarian Wound Questionnaire a therapeutic experience.

4 I have not presumed that everything respondents reported is gospel. I had no desire to include some sort of "lie scale" or other test of respondents' veracity, even if such an inclusion were possible. I think this rather mimics therapy or coaching, where helpers take the studied stance of not doubting or disputing their clients' reports, especially in the beginning, when relationship forming is going on, and typically not until they discover that they must, because their client's story isn't hanging together, sounds classically delusional, and so on. I take the fact that respondents are only telling their story, as opposed to the

"whole truth" or a rounded picture of reality, as no bigger (or smaller) a problem than the equivalent problem one encounters in session.

5 As many respondents identified their mother (or some other female, like their grandmother) as being the authoritarian in their family as identified their father (or some other male). The same was true with respect to work, where as many respondents reported authoritarian female bosses as reported authoritarian male bosses. Again, this is not a scientific study and I have no statistics or statistical analysis to present. But I did find this result interesting and surprising – at first glance. At second glance, it helps explain why women can be as staunchly fascistic as men when fascism gets a toehold in society. Needless to say, I am not suggesting that women are more authoritarian than men or even as a rule as authoritarian as men. What it does mean is that women are not exempt from any discussions about who does the wounding.

6 There are obvious differences between experiencing authoritarian victimization in childhood, say at the hands of a parent, stepparent, or grandparent, and experiencing that victimization as an adult, say at the hands of a boyfriend, girlfriend, husband, or wife. In the first instance, we understand why the child could not just leave. In the second instance, we have to wonder why that adult stayed. Respondents wonder that too! This is the result that perhaps surprised me the most: how often victims of authoritarian wounding in childhood went on to choose one, or a series, of authoritarian mates. One clear takeaway from this pattern is that, when your client reports that his or her current mate is an authoritarian, you will want to check in on what is probably a history of childhood trauma and wounding.

7 A note on methodology. I think that the method I employed, by allowing respondents to define "authoritarianism" as they saw fit, is both interesting and legitimate.

I put no ideas into their head; I didn't define my terms for them, thus begging the question; I made no insinuations as to what harm or negative results they might have experienced. I mentioned nothing about political, cultural, or religious affiliations. Rather, I wanted to do something in keeping with the precepts of linguistic philosophy: to let people describe a phenomenon in their own way and to see what similarities and commonalities emerged. What we have, operating this way, is not a textbook or dictionary definition of "authoritarianism" but many poignant, powerful descriptions that amount to a tableau or tapestry. I think that this is one perfectly legitimate approach to learning about human nature and human affairs.

8 I think it would be sensible to formally add authoritarian wounding to our current list of adverse childhood experiences. The adverse childhood experience literature has focused on ten adverse experiences that contribute to long-term psychological and emotional difficulties: physical abuse, sexual abuse, emotional abuse, physical neglect, emotional neglect, violence toward the mother, household substance abuse, household mental illness, parental separation or divorce, and the incarceration of a household member. But many other adverse childhood experiences likewise produce negative psychological and emotional consequences. I think that we should consider adding authoritarian contact and wounding to the list of significant adverse childhood experiences.

9 I would have loved to learn more about the following, which in hindsight would have been valuable areas to inquire about. I would have loved to learn about cross-cultural differences. It may well be the case that what may look like authoritarian behavior may be an artifact of culture. If your whole society is strict in certain ways, say with respect to modest dress, or if your whole society highly prizes a certain value, like education in Confucian philosophy, then it follows that many members of that society

may be "strict" and "tough" in these regards without being full-fledged authoritarian personalities. Likewise, I would also have loved to learn more about the negative effects of cataclysmic societal circumstances. For example, to what extent are South Korea's epidemic mental health problems, including multigenerational authoritarian wounding, a consequence of living in an armed state across from a hostile neighbor for more than half a century? I would have loved to learn more in both of these two fascinating areas of inquiry.

10 It turned out that to a person, nothing had really fully worked to help victims heal their authoritarian wounds or resolve the consequences of their traumatic experiences. Most aspired to healing, made efforts at healing, and were still hopeful about healing, but knew that they were not "there" yet – typically not by a long shot. Many expressed the belief that they would never fully heal. To my mind, this means the following for helpers. First, many of your clients may be deeply pessimistic about the possibility that they will get any real help from you, given that they believe that they are broken, ruined, or doomed. Second, for those clients who retain some hope of healing and who see themselves on a journey of healing, they will deeply appreciate examining these issues, even if that examination proves painful, and are already primed to see this healing journey as a long one. They may prove very patient and very accepting of small gains, given their understanding of how severely they've been wounded.

11 For those of you who are both helpers and also researchers and/or writers of books, I recommend the "easy research" path that I pursued. The methodology is simple. You create a questionnaire (or some other sort of instrument), you post it (on your website or somewhere else where respondents can access it), you announce its existence and invite others to announce its existence, and you then "enjoy" the results. Does this methodology come with its flaws and

shortcomings? Of course, it does. But it also produces rich results without, it should be added, requiring any grant proposals, funding efforts, or institutional hoops. Personally, I think that this brand of "qualitative research" (which is too fancy a way of describing it) might become your research method of choice. It has a lot to recommend it.

12 I hadn't thought of the possibility of respondents identifying the authoritarian in their life as their own adult child. This was an interesting finding to me. While this response was much rarer than respondents identifying a parent or a mate, it came up often enough to represent its own interesting finding. And when it did come up, respondents seemed particularly pained and perplexed, in large measure because they had to grapple with the possibility that they were somehow instrumental in creating this authoritarian. Since many of your clients may be in the age range where they have both aging parents and adult children, and since some of them may be dealing with a living authoritarian in both categories, this is a possibility worth investigating with clients.

13 I found that most respondents produced quite sophisticated responses: for instance, in thinking through whether they considered the authoritarian in their life more an authoritarian leader or more an authoritarian follower (or both, depending typically on whether the authoritarian was at home, where he or she led, or in the world, where he or she followed). One thing this finding suggests to me is that we shouldn't automatically predict that clients can't deal with nuanced distinctions or complex ideas. It may of course be the case that respondents to my questionnaire were a self-selected group of individuals who were able to think at the level required of the questionnaire. But it nevertheless makes sense not to presume that a given client can't go deep or do subtle work with you.

14 It was rather painful reading and transcribing these stories. Imagine living them! I think that, as helpers, we

can inadvertently not credit our clients with having lived through an awful lot (even if we ourselves did!). Because the current dominant paradigm has us scanning for symptoms of disorders rather than exploring our clients' life experiences, we can easily forget that life hurts and that our clients may have come to us because they have been harmed. I think that these real respondent stories are extremely valuable in reminding us of these realities.

15 While we do not know where these millions upon millions of authoritarians come from, ready at what amounts to the drop of a hat to administer massive electroshock to their fellow human beings in "learning experiments," to feverishly follow a fascist, or to treat their children barbarically, they are right at this moment doing their damage behind closed doors. When circumstances allow, they are also doing that same damage brazenly in public. Because there are so many of them – researchers estimate that they may amount to as much as 25% of the population – the amount of harm they do is monumental. Whole societies have reaped the whirlwind, as have countless families.

Respondents by their answers have shed a great deal of light on these many authoritarians. I hope that this book has provided you with some insights into the phenomenon of authoritarian wounding, alerted you to the harm done to many of your clients, pointed out that to learn about this harm you may have to initiate the conversation, and provided you with some tools and strategies to use in your work with victims of authoritarian contact. To be in touch with me, please drop me a line at ericmaisel@hotmail.com and to learn more about the work I do, please visit me at ericmaisel.com. Thank you for reading!

APPENDIX

AUTHORITARIAN WOUND QUESTIONNAIRE

Below is how the Authoritarian Wound Questionnaire appeared (and appears) on my website. When I speak throughout the book about respondents to the questionnaire, this is the questionnaire to which I'm referring.

**

Authoritarian Wound Questionnaire

I'm currently researching a book with the working title *Healing the Authoritarian Wound*. I would love to have your contribution to this book. You can help me (and others) by taking the below Authoritarian Wound Questionnaire. Just copy the questions, provide your answers (at whatever length you like), and send them along to me at ericmaisel@hotmail.com. By providing me with your answers you understand that I may use what you've written in a forthcoming book. Just let me know how you'd like to be identified: real first name and last initial or made-up first name and last initial.

I think the extent to which folks have been harmed by contact with an authoritarian parent, other authoritarian family member, authoritarian social or cultural figure (like the leader of the church into which they were born), authoritarian in the workplace, or other "close" authoritarian, has been largely ignored or explored only tangentially in other contexts (as, for example, with regard to an "authoritarian parenting style"). Given research estimates as to the number of authoritarians out there, probably virtually everybody has been harmed by contact with an authoritarian personality. You may be in this very large group.

By "authoritarian wound" I mean the wound created by having been raised by, having to live with, or having to deal with someone with an "authoritarian personality." There isn't actually a single "authoritarian personality" ("authoritarian leaders" and "authoritarian followers" differ in important ways) and there's lots to say on this subject. But I'm going to trust that you have an excellent intuitive grasp of what an authoritarian looks like and what harm he or she can do without me having to paint a specific picture or provide any explanations.

Please send your responses to me directly to ericmaisel@hotmail.com. There is no pressing deadline on this but of course I'd love to get your answers sooner rather than later. Feel free to skip any questions that don't move you or that don't pertain you. Of course, you may not have the time to do this, as there are only a million other things you might be doing. But it may strike you as personally useful and even important to tackle this. So, I hope that you will contribute. Thank you!

**

Authoritarian Wound Questionnaire

1 Have you had the experience of having to deal with an "authoritarian personality": a parent, sibling, mate, adult child, spiritual leader, coworker, boss, etc.?
2 What was that experience (or those experiences) like?
3 Authoritarian personalities are typically described as either "authoritarian leaders" or "authoritarian followers." What's your intuition as to whether the authoritarian in your life was more an "authoritarian leader" or more an "authoritarian follower"? Why do you think that?
4 Sometimes an authoritarian parent is described as "having an authoritarian parenting style." Which seems truer to you, if the authoritarian you're discussing is a parent: that he or she had an "authoritarian personality" or an

"authoritarian parenting style"? That is, was the person in question more an authoritarian "through and through" or did it seem like he or she was adopting a particular "parenting style"?

5. What would you say were the personal consequences of having been wounded by an authoritarian? (There are many common consequences but I don't want to name them, as that will "put ideas in your head." I'd rather you think through what you believe those consequences to have been.)
6. What (if anything) has helped you deal with or heal from this "authoritarian wound"?
7. If you've been in therapy or counseling, has the issue of "dealing with an authoritarian personality" come up and been addressed? Has therapy or counseling helped in this regard?
8. If you've received a "mental disorder" diagnosis of any sort, do you see any relationship between having been wounded by an authoritarian and the symptoms that led to that "mental disorder" diagnosis?
9. If you had to make a complete break with the authoritarian in your life, what effect did that have on you, either positive (e.g., you felt safer and saner) or negative (e.g., feelings of loss and guilt)?
10. If you are still dealing with an authoritarian, what (if anything) helps you cope?
11. What advice would you like to share with those individuals who, like yourself, have been wounded in this way?
12. Please add anything you'd like to include about living with, working with, or dealing with an authoritarian and/or healing (or not healing) from the authoritarian wound.

Thank you!

Please email your responses to me at ericmaisel@hotmail.com

**

INDEX

Aabida's story 73
Adam's story 59–60
addiction consequences: Adele's story 132–6; Harold's story 130–2
Adele's story 78–82, 132–6
Adorno, Theodor 1, 2; *The Authoritarian Personality* 26, 74
Adult Children of Alcoholics therapy 116
adverse childhood experiences 7–8
affirmations and prayers 126
aggression cluster 2, 9–11, 24; anger 11; assaultive behavior 12; cruelty 11; destructiveness 13; domination 15; hatred 11; low agreeableness 14; punishment 12; quixotic and unclear rules 15–16; readiness and impulsivity 14; rigidity and obsession with control 13; sadism 15; threats and scare tactics 12–13; violence 12
agreeableness 14
Alfred's story 57, 193–4
Alice's story 20, 64, 189–90
Altemeyer, Bob 2, 6; "Authoritarianism, Religious Fundamentalism, Quest, and Prejudice" 70

"Always stand up to authoritarians" 195
Amelia's story 194
anger 11, 86, 151
Anna's story 93, 139–40
Anne's story 83–6; on religiosity 74
anti-education environment 63, 66–7
anti-intellectualism 56–7, 61–8
anti-intraception 2
antiracism 117
anti-rationalism 56–7, 61–8
anti-thinking environment 65
anxiety management 22; affirmations and prayers 126; analysis 123; attitude choice 122; behavioral changes 123–4; ceremonies and rituals 126; cognitive work 124; deep breathing 124; discharge techniques 128; disidentification techniques 125–6; existential decisiveness 121–2; guided imagery 125; improved appraising 122–3; incanting 124; lifestyle support 123; mindfulness techniques 125; personality upgrading 122; pharmaceuticals 128; physical

relaxation techniques 125; preparation techniques 127; recovery work 128–9; reorienting techniques 127; symptom confrontation techniques 127
appraising situations, anxiety management 122–3
Arendt, Hannah 94
assaultive behavior 12, 48
attitude choice, anxiety management 122
auditory processing disorder 114
Audrey's story 152
Australian Department of Health and Ageing 171
"Authoritarianism, Religious Fundamentalism, Quest, and Prejudice" (Altemeyer) 70
authoritarian parenting 2–3, 114; alert for triggers 192; attitudes and behaviors 189–90; contrary vision 193–4; creating support system 191–2; exorcising guilt and shame 190; healthy/sane family members 192–3; Karen's story 32–8; Laura's story 46–50; limiting contact 194; Monica's story 39–42; Paula's story 50–2; physical separation 188–9; psychological separation 189; Sarah's story 42–5; testing careful compassion 191
authoritarian personality 1; characteristics of 2; dark triad of personality traits 6; respondents' perception 3–4
The Authoritarian Personality (Adorno) 26, 74

authoritarian's love of chaos and disasters 59–60
authoritarian victimization 204
authoritarian wounding 144, 156–7; avoidance and reluctance 163; client's childhood experiences 158; diagnose-and-treat model 163; diagnosing mental disorders 158; healing process 159; historical investigation 159–60; internal guiding question 164; pseudo-medical model 162; questions to clients 160–1; relationship 181; *see also* victims of authoritarian wounding
Authoritarian Wound Questionnaire 3, 28, 112, 119, 203, 209–11
average authoritarians 5
Ayanna's story 57

"banality of evil" 94
Bath, Howard 169
Baumrind, Diana 2
behavioral changes, anxiety management 123–4
belief system 22, 43; religious 75–6
A Better National Health Service (Tomlinson) 165–6
A Better NHS (Tomlinson) 169
bigotries 58
Bob's story 141–3
British National Health Service 137

CBT training 134, 142, 190
ceremonies and rituals, anxiety management 126
coercion, demands and 93

INDEX

cognitive work, anxiety management 124
compassion 94
Confucian philosophy 205–6
Conradi, Lisa 166
conscience, narcissistic authoritarian's lack of 94
conventionalism 2, 95, 98–104
cowardice 95
cruelty 11
cynicism 2, 59

dark triad, of personality traits 6, 54
Deborah's story 57–8
deception 60
deep breathing, anxiety management 124
demands: and coercion 93; loyalty 96–7
Denise's story 153–4, 198–9
depression consequences: Joanne's story 112–18; mental disorder paradigm 112
derision 55
destructiveness 2, 13
diagnose-and-treat model 163
diagnosing mental disorders 158
diminishment 57–8
discharge techniques 128
disidentification techniques, anxiety management 125–6
Dolores' story 21
domination 15, 93–4

eggshell-walking 25–31
egotism 90–1
Eichmann, Adolph 94
Elizabeth's story 196–7

Ellen's story 95
Emily's story 91, 93–4
emotional separation, Maria's story 200–1
empathy 94
The Encyclopedia of Social Work 166–7
enemies' lists 91
existential care *see* existentialism
existential decisiveness, anxiety management 121–2
existential-informed care 179
existentialism: authentic living 174; cosmic indifference 176; definition of 173; human energy 175; inviting clients 177–80; power of microbes 176; tenets of 174
exploitation cluster: anti-intellectualism 56–7; bigotries 58; cynicism 59; deception 60; derides 55; diminishment 57–8; hypocrisy 57; intrusiveness 54; love of chaos and disasters 59–60; manipulation 54–5; prejudices 58; preoccupation with sex and promiscuity 58–9; religiosity 56; ridicules 55; shames 55

"A Face and a Name: Civil Victims of Insurgent Groups in Iraq" 62
family dynamics: bravery 181, 184–7; strength 181–4
fascism 72

Gentile, Emilio 72
grandiosity 90–1

guided imagery, anxiety management 125
guilt, absence of 94

Harold's story 130–2
hate-and-punish agenda 9, 10, 16, 55
hate-punish-and-conceal agenda 99
hatred 11, 20
Healing the Addictive Personality (Jampolsky) 154
Healing the Authoritarian Wound 209
healthy narcissism 100
Henry's story 92–3
Herculean effort 175
Highly Sensitive Person (HSP) 197
hypocrisy 57

ignorance 61–8
impulsive aggression 14
incantations, anxiety management 124
"The Influence of the Concept of Authoritarian Personality Today" (Smolik) 99
Ingrid's story 153
intrusiveness 54
"Is There a Link Between Religiosity and Authoritarianism?" (Perry) 71

Jennifer's story 193
Jill's story 54
Joanne's story 113–18
Jonathan's story 67–8

Karen's story 32–8
Kezelman, Cathy 171, 172

Larry's story 56
Laura's story 46–50
learning 67, 114; disability 79, 81; experiments 1, 6, 208
Lea's story 152–3
Lee's story 154–5
Leslie's story 92, 199–200
lifestyle supports, anxiety management 123
Lippincott Nursing Center blog 167
"Living the Questions" 168
Lois's story 102–3
low agreeableness 14
loyalty demands 96–7

machiavellianism 54
Madeline's story 96–7
"Manifesto of Futurist Sacred Art" 72
manipulation, authoritarianism and 54–5; Adele's story 78–82
Margaret's story 64–5
Maria's story 86–9, 103–4, 191–2, 200–1
Marinetti 72
Mark's story 63–4, 94, 189
Markway, Barbara 168
Marvin's story 192
Maryanne's story 190
Matt's story 60
Max's story 96
Melanie's story 140–1
mental disorder diagnoses 135
mental disorder paradigm 112
mental health profession 165
Milgram, Stanley 1, 6
military, exploiting institutions 69

INDEX

mindfulness techniques, anxiety management 125
Miriam's story 120–1
Monica's story 39–42
Motherless Daughters 148
Mussolini 72, 75
mythic determination 92–3

narcissism cluster: absence of guilt 94; coercion 93; compassion 94; conventionalism 95; cowardice 95; demands 93; domination, need for 93–4; egotism 90–1; empathic skills 94; enemies' lists 91; grandiosity 90–1; healthy narcissism 100; "hollow" narcissism 98; lack of conscience 94; loyalty demands 96–7; mythic determination 92–3; paranoia 91; social status 95; submissiveness 95; superficial charm 95; superstitions 92–3; truth, held as enemy 91–2; unacknowledged anxiety 92; unhealthy narcissism 100
Nausea 175
"Never stand up to authoritarians" 195

paranoia 91
passive authoritarians 10
passivity–conventionality–narcissism triad 104
Paula's story 50–2
Pence, Donna 166
Perry, Philip 71
personality upgrade 122

pharmaceuticals, anxiety management 128
Phillip's story 92
physical complaints: Anna's story 139–40; Bob's story 141–3; Melanie's story 140–1; mind/body connection 137; trauma-informed physical care 137–8
physical relaxation techniques 125
physical separation: Denise's story 198–9; Elizabeth's story 196–7; Leslie's story 199–200; overview of 195–6; Regina's story 197–8
plane geometry 67
"political religion" 72
post-traumatic stress disorder (PTSD) 116, 166
Practice Guidelines for the Treatment of Complex Trauma (Kezelman & Stavropoulos) 171
prejudices 58
preoccupation with sex and promiscuity 58–9
preparation techniques, anxiety management 127
Priscilla's story 100–1
PTSD *see* post-traumatic stress disorder (PTSD)
punishment(s) 12, 72; rules and 17–24

Rachel's story 73
Ralph's story 54–5
Raymond's story 151–2
readiness to aggress 14, 25–31
recovery work, anxiety management 128–9

INDEX

Regina's story 197–8
"Religion and Prejudice: The Role of Religious Fundamentalism, Quest, and Right-Wing Authoritarianism" (Hunsberger & Laurier) 70
religiosity 56, 69–76
reorienting techniques 127
repetition compulsion, Roberta's story 144–50
ridicules 55
right-wing authoritarianism 2
Roberta's story 58–9, 144–50
Robert's story 101–2
Rob's story 55
robust anxiety management 119
rule-breakers 17–24
rules 7; and aggression 15–16; and punishment 17–24; quixotic and unclear 15–16, 19; reasons for 22; as weapons 24

sadism 15
Samantha's story 55
Sarah's story 42–5
Sara's story 53
scare tactics 12–13
Schnur, Myrna 167
sexism 40, 43
shaming efforts 55
Smolik, Josef 99–100
social status 95
Stavropoulos, Pam 171, 172
The Stranger 175
submissiveness 2, 95, 99–100
superficial charm 95
superstitions 92–3

Susan's story 95
symptom confrontation techniques 127

threats 12–13
The Three Pillars of Trauma-Informed Care (Bath) 169
Tomlinson, Jonathan 165, 169
trauma-informed care: approaches, principles and practices of 167–8; client safety issues 169; dissociative responses 171; issues as human results 170–1; mental health profession 165, 166; recognize breadth of functioning 169–70; special care around boundary issues 171–2
trauma-informed physical care 137–8
traumatic events 7–8, 17, 50
truth, held as enemy 91–2
two-faced authoritarian 5–6

unacknowledged anxiety 92
unhealthy narcissism 100

victims of authoritarian wounding 4, 24, 61, 181, 202–8; Laura's story 46–50; Paula's story 50–2
violation of rules 17–24
violent behavior 12
Vivien's story 105–11

walking on eggshells 25–31
Wilson, Chase 166

Zachary's story 91

For Product Safety Concerns and Information please contact our EU representative GPSR@taylorandfrancis.com
Taylor & Francis Verlag GmbH, Kaufingerstraße 24, 80331 München, Germany

www.ingramcontent.com/pod-product-compliance
Lightning Source LLC
Chambersburg PA
CBHW051356290426
44108CB00015B/2042